THE NEXT 50 YEARS:

A Prophetic Perspective

Russell Walden

Copyright © 2016 Russell Walden
All rights reserved.

ISBN: 1533214220
ISBN 13: 9781533214225

To My Wife, Kitty:
Without you, none of this would be possible.

TABLE OF CONTENTS

Introduction   vii

Chapter 1	A 50 Year Political Shift	1
Chapter 2	God's 500 Year Step	8
Chapter 3	African American Promotion Continues	15
Chapter 4	A Coming Hispanic Majority	24
Chapter 5	24 Coming Events	29
Chapter 6	A New Great Awakening!	36
Chapter 7	An Openly Gay President	47
Chapter 8	Natural Disasters	56
Chapter 9	The Union Threatened	60
Chapter 10	The Republican Party Chastised	65
Chapter 11	Arabic Apostles are Coming	70
Chapter 12	Ethnic Justice Prevails in the Earth	75
Chapter 13	Shifting White Majority	80
Chapter 14	An African-American Elite	86
Chapter 15	From White Privilege to Servant Sons	92
Chapter 16	A Land Invasion of the U.S.	100
Chapter 17	Revival in Europe	107
Chapter 18	Payment of Africa's Love Debt to the UK	113
Chapter 19	Radical Spiritual Shift in the US and Europe	119

Chapter 20	Islam will be Marginalized	124
Chapter 21	A Comprehensive Overview	128

Conclusion 133

INTRODUCTION

Over the last year God moved upon me to write a prophetic perspective of the next fifty years. He impressed me with 24 specific events that are coming on the scene over the next five decades that will change our world and affect us both personally and corporately in the church and Christian culture. Over and over in prayer the voice of God came clearly:

> *"You must SAY what you SEE.... you must say what you see for I will reveal the fullness of My purposes in the earth for the next fifty years".*

These were the words that the Father spoke within the acoustics of my inner man. I was sitting in a meeting in Hollister, Missouri where an apostle to Africa (Warren Hunter) was speaking. As he spoke the anointing filled the room where only a handful were in attendance. I had always said that this man standing at the lectern was one of the best kept secrets in the Midwest because when he went to Africa he commanded audiences of 10's of 1000's but in America he seemed to garner little interest. The spirit of God flowed over me and lifted my thoughts into areas of contemplation that had nothing to do with the message the speaker was giving. I had learned long ago that when the anointing is genuine and your ears are open that God will often teach you and show you many things unconnected with the words of the speaker because the heavens are open and the scrolls of revelation are unfurled. The Lord spoke again – "take your phone out and begin to take these notes..." I took out my iPhone and opened the note-taking app. This was a far cry from John at Patmos scrawling on papyrus in the murky light of the cave where he had been banished.

> *"I'm going to give you 24 things that will happen in the next fifty years – so that My people who are called by My name will not be uninformed but believing in the midst of that which is to come."*

Then as Warren continued speaking I didn't hear a word he said but in the anointing and presence of God in that room I recorded what God gave me, typing on the awkward keyboard of my iPhone the 24 things that God spoke, one right after another. In a few minutes as the service carried on I touched my wife Kitty's sleeve and handed her my phone – open to the notes the Father had dictated. As she silently read I watched her face flush and her eyebrows head into the territory of the incredulous. The Lord was speaking. The curtain of time and happenstance was standing open and through a glass darkly, knowing in part and seeing in part events were portended that stupefied the mind. This is the writing you hold in your hand and my expectation is that you will find it a reverent presentation of the subjective unfolding of things hinted at by the voice of the Father I have followed my entire life.

This book is not a diatribe or the ramblings of an eccentric ideologue. It is a faithful report of those things the Lord revealed to Me in the same subjective manner that He speaks to all of us – even you. Among other things in this book we will explore the purposes of God on the national scene that transcend any political agenda or cultural ideology. God is not a Republican; neither is he a Democrat! In fact, to the relief of our Western European friends we have discovered that neither is God an American. As humorous as this statement might seem it is so important to adjust our thinking to a kingdom mentality else we become pawns of a political process and lose our effectiveness in the earth even as Jesus said regarding the salt that loses its savor. The timeframe covered in these things that God has revealed spans half a century.

Most prophets today absolutely avoid and consider it unsafe and immature to give timeframes. I couldn't agree more. In the years of prophetic ministry and speaking into the lives of thousands I have given many time frames and deep specifics. I always pause before doing so and give the caveat that no matter how anointed the prophet may be they only see through a glass darkly and in part. Trust me I know I can "miss it" and I know I can "MISS IT". Having said that quite frankly I have seldom been wrong. Things that God has given me for people they have found years later that events played out as the Father revealed, in the sequence and timing that He spoke. This writing is no different – but know this that the sequence and timings expressed here can only be held up to the scrutiny of future history played out and the point is not that I as a prophet can be right or wrong but rather that God be glorified. The whole purpose of the prophetic is not to be right or accurate first of all but to bring others closer to Jesus and to who He desires to be to you and through you and in you. Prophets are not psychics or clairvoyants and we should not regard them as such though this is the prevailing attitude among many.

The things that God showed me included seasons of trial and also outpouring for the church. There will be a great setback for the church in the earth - specifically the Evangelical church on the world scene regarding its perceived influence and power to shape global issues and culture. Many will see this as the work of the devil however it is rather the hand of God bringing about a purpose unexplored and unforeseen by the shallow, tone deaf, politically manipulated Christian electorate in the western nations. This difficulty will be termed by the church looking back in history as "the Great Disillusionment".

> *From the ashes of this season will emerge a new great awakening that will roll back the clock and bring humanity itself away from the abyss of impending judgment that so many have seen and prognosticate it so vociferously.*

From far-flung parts of the world never known for evangelistic fervor will emerge a youthful generation of apostolic evangelists who will sell their lives cheap for the cause of Christ. Even in the U.S. young people armed only with their bibles and their passports will board airlines to Jihadist countries and lay down their lives for the gospel much to the chagrin of the Establishment Church. Your task will be to know these men and women when they come on the scene and not to reject them because they have not arisen from well-known churches, nor will recognized movements or denominations sanction them.

> *[Joel 2:1-2] 1 Blow ye the trumpet in Zion, and sound an alarm in my holy mountain: let all the inhabitants of the land tremble: for the day of the LORD cometh, for [it is] nigh at hand; 2 A day of darkness and of gloominess, a day of clouds and of thick darkness, as the morning spread upon the mountains: a great people and a strong; there hath not been ever the like, neither shall be any more after it, [even] to the years of many generations.*

You can see as Joel 2:1-2 predicts – the years ahead will be a season of gloom, clouds and darkness – YES but also as *"morning spread on the mountains...*" As you read through this book know this - - that THE SKY ISN'T FALLING the KINGDOM IS COMING! In nothing shall we dismayed or dis-spirited for the kingdoms of this world are becoming the kingdoms of our God and His Christ! Having said that, know also that there will be shaking and there will be change – uncomfortable changes in the earth attended by a simultaneous upswing of cataclysm and natural disaster even as Jesus said in many places in the gospel would occur in the end times. However, the end is not yet because our end is not in disaster and darkness but in the establishment of God's purposes on the earth and through His children as He raises up a generation of nation-confronting believers who will birth the final testimonial of redemption to mankind through the sacrifice of Christ.

What is the timing of these things and by what right do I as the author or ANY writer or speaker claim to be in receipt of such precognitive information? In Matthew chapter 24 we find Jesus prophesying about the day that you and I live in, referring to the nation of Israel as a fig tree. He said that when the fig tree puts forth leaves that humanity will be in a time of great shift from the dispensation of man to the economy of God come to earth.

> *[Mat 24:32-34 KJV] 32 Now learn a parable of the fig tree; When his branch is yet tender, and putteth forth leaves, ye know that summer [is] nigh: 33 So likewise ye, when ye shall see all these things, know that it is near, [even] at the doors. 34 Verily I say unto you, This generation shall not pass, till all these things be fulfilled.*

Notice in verse 34 he says that this generation shall not pass away before these things would be fulfilled. What things are we talking about? In 1948 the nation of Israel was restored as a nation. The fig tree for centuries has been a symbol of the national identity of the people of God. Measuring from 1948 assuming this is the generation that Jesus spoke of, how long is a generation? Some believe that a generation biblically is 20 years. Some believe that a generation is 40, 60 or some other arbitrary length of time. Understanding God's reckoning of time is helpful to us.

God calculates two types of time: linear time and fullness of time or in the Greek *Chronos or Kairos*. In this writing you will see that God gives us a very clear understanding of his measurement of a linear generation. However, many have gotten into trouble trying to predict apocalyptic events based on some empirical measurement extracted from a scriptural formula. This is not what you will see in this book. In this book we will deal more with *fullness of time* or in the Greek *Kairos Timing* and the shifting of human history from the dispensation of man to the economy of God ushered in through a redeemed people cooperating with God's broader purposes in the kingdom.

Is it even valid or legitimate to look into the Scriptures or other portents as the Magi scanning the night sky to divine the return of mankind's Savior? The prophet Amos declared under divine inspiration that there is nothing God will do in the earth that will not first be enunciated by the prophets and that includes His timings.

> *[Amo 3:7 KJV] 7 Surely the Lord GOD will do nothing, but he revealeth his secret unto his servants the prophets.*

Who are the prophets then? The majority opinion in Christianity is that prophets no longer exist. The commonly held doctrine of ceassationism maintains that prophets are no longer necessary because we are in possession of the Holy Scripture as penned by New Testament writers. The pretext for this assertion is found in Paul's first letter to the Corinthians:

> *[1Co 13:10 KJV] 10 But when that which is perfect is come, then that which is in part shall be done away.*

The question I put to those who think this way is if the Bible is perfect then why do we have so many translations? Where are the original manuscripts otherwise known as the autographs? In the first century church the primitive believers were likewise in possession of an infallible body of Scriptures (i.e. the Old Testament). Was the Old Testament in some way fallible and therefore apostles, prophets, etc., were needed to bring the church forward? Is the New Testament somehow MORE INSPIRED than the Old Testament in such a way that the Old Testament times called for prophets but the New Testament era once inaugurated does not? Why then were apostles and prophets necessary then? And if they were necessary then in light of the fact that these believers held Holy Scriptures in their custody and yet needed apostles and prophets as well as pastors, etc. why then do we not need them now? I submit to you that we do in fact need the office of the prophet and that prophets are in the earth. Indeed, if prophets are in the earth then it is true of modern day prophets according to the words of Amos that God is revealing to them the very secret of His cosmic purposes on the grand scale of human history.

Who are the prophets? They are those called just as pastors and evangelists (who are accepted by the Establishment church) are likewise called. Not only that but all of God's people are a prophetic people. Lest we see a person in the office of the prophet as a member of an elite core with secret information unavailable to the rest of us let us remember the words of Paul in 1 Corinthians 14:31

[1Co 14:31 KJV] 31 For ye may all prophesy one by one, that all may learn, and all may be comforted.

There are many prophets in the earth today and in fact God has released upon the earth and upon the people of God - the redeemed, a prophetic spirit through which they can perceive God's purposes and articulate them to an incredulous humanity. Why do you think as Jesus predicted there would be so many false prophets in the earth?

> *[Mat 24:11 KJV] 11 And many false prophets shall rise, and shall deceive many.*

There are false prophets abounding in the earth today as the implementation of the strategy of Satan to resist the plan of God in raising up many true prophets, men and women in the rank-and-file of the redeemed and those who stand in the office of the prophet no less than an equivalent to men such as Isaiah, Ezekiel, and the other examples from Scripture we have and can cite. With this in mind you will find this book unashamedly prophetic speaking of events yet to come over the next many decades with an authority not drawn from popular opinion but from the anointing and unction of prophetic office executed in behalf of those who have an ear to hear what the Spirit would say to the churches.

CHAPTER 1
A 50 YEAR POLITICAL SHIFT

In 2008 during the presidential election season God began to speak to me about His will being carried out in the political process - to the disappointment of the conservative Christian electorate. President Obama would win the election. Any God called prophetic voice could see this and knew it to be true at the time no matter how disappointing it may have been to many. I was abashed at the reticence of the prophets to say what they saw in regard to the outcome of the presidential election. Anyone who was listening to the prophets in the pre-election season in 2008 and reading between the lines knew God had clearly revealed to established and mature prophetic voices that Barack Obama would win the election defeating candidate Mitt Romney as in fact happened. Well-known prophetic ministers in their broadcasts and their writings obviously were skirting the issue and declining to speak openly about what they saw as an Obama victory. What possible motive could a prophet have for not saying what they see?

The prophetic movement which is an offshoot of the Charismatic/Pentecostal renewal is predominantly conservative and Republican in its political leanings. Without impugning the integrity or motive of any particular ministry - the timidity of national prophetic leaders to speak boldly and honestly about Obama's victory could very well have arisen from the concern or outright fear of being rejected and defunded by their conservative constituency and supporters if they had done so. In this book you will see why God Himself put Barack Obama in office. Man can pull the voting lever but God decides the outcome (Prov. 16:33). This thinking is repugnant to the voting public of any nation under a representative government. It has been said that the thought or concept of the sovereignty of God over the affairs of man is the "cod liver oil" of Christian culture. What do I mean by this? Does not the voting public have the last word in any election? The prophet Daniel speaking by the spirit of God clearly stipulated:

> *Dan. 2:21 He changes the times and the seasons;* **_He removes kings and sets up kings._** *He gives wisdom to the wise and knowledge to those who have understanding! 22 He reveals the deep and secret things; He knows what is in the darkness, and the light dwells with Him!*

You as a believer are both a citizen of the kingdom and a citizen of your nation of residence. It is irresponsible for you not to participate in the political process, casting your vote as an informed citizen. Your perspective however on the outcome of any particular election certainly must not exclude the truth of Daniel 2:21 which plainly indicates that your vote cast and the outcome of the issues at hand are not determined in electoral precincts but in the throne room of God. Therefore, when Barack Obama gained the White House in 2008 and subsequently re-elected in 2012 - we can only say *"the Lord gives and the Lord takes away – Blessed be the name of the Lord!"* Unfortunately, this was not the posture of Evangelical, Charismatic, or Pentecostal Christianity as a whole in the last two presidential election cycles. The church, particularly the Evangelical Church has been, in recent decades seduced by the political process and reduced to nothing more than a voting block or pawn of a jaded and corrupt conservative political party specifically the RNC, a party which has demonstrated every intention for over 30 years to renege on the promises made to a gullible Christian electorate solely for the purpose getting in office and staying in power.

God is warning the church and Christianity at large that He is a jealous God and will not sit idly by as his people put their expectations on man looking to the political process to accomplish what only God Himself, and faith in God can bring about. A similar situation took place in Isaiah's day when Israel faced the invasion of a foreign army and looked to the nation of Assyria for protection rather than trusting in God. The warning of God through Isaiah chastised the people and predicted that the very nation they put their trust in would eventually overwhelm and devastate them nationally:

[Isa 8:6-8 KJV] 6 Forasmuch as this people refuseth the waters of Shiloah that go softly, and rejoice in Rezin and Remaliah's son; 7 Now therefore, behold, the Lord bringeth up upon them the waters of the river, strong and many, [even] the king of Assyria, and all his glory: and he shall come up over all his channels, and go over all his banks: 8 And he shall pass through Judah; he shall overflow and go over, he shall reach [even] to the neck; and the stretching out of his wings shall fill the breadth of thy land, O Immanuel.

The church has prostituted itself to the political process by looking to the Republican National Convention and conservative leaning candidates to bring about justice and righteousness by adjudicating and legislating in behalf of the conservative Christian political agenda. From the days of Ronald Reagan until now the RNC has pandered to the hot button issues of the Christian electorate, promising change if only the church specifically the Evangelical church would back them in an upcoming election. The false promises were made and then once Reagan and successive political candidates over the years attained political office denied them without the church's help, they would then abandon every promise they had made to the Christian conservative voting demographic. When called to account for their treachery Republican candidates now firmly in office would simply exclaim *"yes we are so sorry we haven't been able to keep our promises, it's the Democrat's fault however – and the answer is four more years!"*

The Father says this – *"The bishop prick of the executive branch of government has been taken from the Republican party and handed over to the Democrats for the next 50 years"*. For 40 of the last 60 years the Republican party has dominated the executive branch of government and held the Oval Office firmly in its grasp. 40 is God's number of testing, proving and also judgment. Consider the following biblical examples:

> 40 days and 40 night's judgment of rain to flood the world and cleanse the earth (Gen. 7:12)
> Moses was on the mountain 40 days (Ex. 24:18)
> 40 days to spy out the promised land (Nu. 14:34)
> Goliath taunted Israel 40 days. (1 Sam. 17:16)
> Ninevah given 40 days to repent (Jonah 3:4-10)
> Jesus fasted 40 days in the wilderness (Mat. 3:17)
> Jesus was seen 40 days after His resurrection (Acts 1:3)

The Republican party has presented itself for decades as the party of God and country. In many circles today Evangelicals and Pentecostal leaning groups and churches consider conservative and Republican values a pre-requisite for being a true believer. I can't tell you how many times in unguarded conversation I've heard conservative believers exclaim "I just can't see how someone can be saved and support the Democratic party…" Just as the Democratic party has co-opted the African American vote, the Women's vote and the LGBT lobby – even so the Republican party has sought in earnest from the days of Ronald Reagan to manipulate the Christian conservative demographic to its own political ends. They obfuscate, lie, make false promises and when called to account blame it on the liberals as the scriptures say "wiping their mouth and claiming they have done nothing wrong..." The difference is this – the Democratic party for all its political machinations has not attempted to brand itself as the party of "God and country..." What the Republican party has done is no different than what the Democrats have done with the exception that they put GOD'S NAME on their corrupt schemes and manipulated GOD'S PEOPLE to their nefarious ends. As the scripture so often says:

"... and the LORD heard it ..."

I hear the Father say ENOUGH is ENOUGH and THAT WILL BE ENOUGH OF THAT. God is neither Republican or Democrat. In fact, God is not even an American (imagine that if you will). As Augustine asserted in his book "The City of God" the value of any form of government including our own is only found in the scope by which it facilitates the spread of the gospel. When Rome became intolerant of the early church God removed them from the face of the earth. In the last many decades the United States and the UK have become intolerant of Christian values and the death knell has been sounded against our form of government. You can plan now to prepare your children and your children's children to live in a VERY DIFFERENT United States and United Kingdom than you have known in your lifetime and the shift will have begun in earnest over the next 50 years.

As the Father spoke these things to me I questioned Him on the details. He said that a liberal woman will come to power in the Oval Office at a time that the country is on the brink of great economic and social distress. She will pull the country back from the precipice of another great economic failure that would pale the 2008 crash by comparison. She will institute tax reform and commerce will thrive. Once again as it was in the day of Bill Clinton, the staggering national deficit will be paid and the country will thrive as it has in years previous. The toll this will take on the credibility of the RNC and Tea Party conservatives will be stunning. She will serve successfully for one term with a split legislative branch dominated by the Republican party. In her second term the Democrats will astonishingly take both the house and the Senate and sweeping liberal reforms will again be passed that will leave the conservative leaning demographic in this country breathless. She will be anything but a lame duck in her second term and show great prowess in domestic as well as foreign affairs. There will be a failed but strongly assertive attempt to pass legislature to allow her to run a third term. This will trigger a constitutional crisis that will be quelled when this lady President will state unequivocally as Lyndon Johnson did at the end of his term that under no circumstances will she accept the nomination of the Democratic party at the end of her second term.

The RNC and their conservative supporters will then throw all of their resources into taking the White House in the next election after the end of this President's tenure. George W. Bush will come out of retirement to direct an all-out campaign to bring the Evangelical Church and the Catholic Church on board in a unified voting constituency in hopes of crushing any thought of the Democrats taking another term. They will fail miserably. The tried and true corrupt political manipulation of the Christian electorate will completely fail and the Democrats will put their candidate – an OPENLY GAY PRESIDENT into the Oval Office by a LANDSLIDE VICTORY.

The church will reel at the stinging blow leveled against them as they realize with shocking intensity the truth of just how ineffective, feeble and out of touch they have become with popular culture and the voting public. This season will be called "the Great Disillusionment". Many churches and denominations once staunchly pro-life and pro-defense of marriage will abandon their conservative values and embrace the LGBT onslaught in hopes of staving off the demise of their organizations. Masses of denominational and nominal Christians will defect from organized religion on a scale that will beggar the current strong movement in that direction even at the present day.

> *In the midst of this chaos and despair the Father says I am bringing forth a new Great Awakening. My people will turn from their false lovers and the lying words of the political influences and will come once again to their knees in prayer. Synods and conferences will be convened across denominational lines on a scale such as has not been seen since the early days of the Charismatic movement in the 60's and 70's. Even in the arena of the business world there will be a resurgence of organizations similar in scope to the Full Gospel Business Men's Fellowship all for the purpose of calling out to Me in prayer. You will pray to Me and I will hear from heaven and heal your land. I will discover the skirts of the wayward bride upon her face and expose the shame with which she has relied on the political and even looking to the military to solve the problems that only My Spirit can address for I say to you:*
>
> *It's not by Might*
>
> *And it's not by Power*
>
> *But it's by My Spirit says the Father that I am going to do the things in the earth that I am going to do.*
>
> *I have told you and told you and told you Oh My People that it isn't your might and it's not your power that is going to do the things in the earth that I'm going to do. I am speaking to you that you must draw yourself away with Me in the secret place where I will reveal to you the wisdom even the hidden wisdom that the knowledgeable and the prudent have rejected. As you come once again into a GLOBAL WORLD-WIDE PRAYER INITIATIVE I will turn the nations and establish godliness again in the land and you will dwell safely with honor and know that I have vouchsafed you and brought you into that which others have said will never be again for I am the Lord your God and I will not be denied.*

CHAPTER 2
GOD'S 500 YEAR STEP

Mankind stands at the threshold of a 500 year sea change. It has been said that God steps through time in 500 year strides. When God revealed the future to Abraham he was made to know that in four generations his progeny would go into captivity in Egypt. This tells us that a generation from God's perspective is 100 years. 430 years later we do in fact see the children of Israel enslaved in Egypt. 480 years after this Solomon completed the first Temple according to the design handed down to him by God. The timeframe between Malachi in the writing of the New Testament was also 480 years approximately to the time when the gospel of Mark and the gospel of Matthew were written. 380 years later the edict of Thessalonica was enforced making Christianity the de facto state religion of the Roman Empire. 480 years after the edict of Thessalonica, Charlemagne had united Western Europe and set the stage for the Christianization of the medieval world. 500 years later after Charlemagne's time John Wickliffe produced the first handwritten manuscript of the Holy Scriptures in the English language. From Wycliffe to the Pentecostal outpouring that began in Los Angeles known as the Azusa Street revival was approximately 500 years. If you measure from the year that Martin Luther nailed his 99 theses to the door of the Wittenberg Chapel in 1517 you will see that another 500 year benchmark is about to be established. We are living in monumental times.

In writing a 50 year perspective from a prophetic standpoint the question always comes: "won't Jesus come back before this time"? We know from the Scriptures that not even Jesus has the answer to this question. He told his disciples that of that day and that hour no man knows not even Jesus himself. This fact gives us insight into the words of Jesus to his disciples in another place where he commanded them: "Occupy, till I come". Jesus said "behold I come quickly..." And yet it's been 2000 years. We are to live in the immediacy of anticipating the return of Jesus at any moment. It may not seem acceptable to some but this is the clear mandate of Scripture. We are to work and serve as though Jesus could come back before you finish reading this sentence, yet you are to plan as though He will not come back for 1000 years. Because the church has not understood this, specifically in the Evangelical church - planning has been limited to the *tactical* whereas *strategic* long-term development has been rejected because after all, "Jesus will come back before then..."

I submit to you that we are living in a period of history that in retrospect by generations future – our time will be compared to the transitional time during which Jesus was born and ultimately crucified and resurrected to the glory of God the Father. Examining events in which Jesus was the focal point we see a prevailing religious system (Judaism) that rejected the Messiah and then an emerging faith that defied definition came forth to take its place. That faith became the church of Acts in the first century and evolved over time into the Christian religion as we know it. Within one generation of the birth of the church the new faith shifted from being a Jewish sect to becoming a wholly Gentile movement completely unrecognizable from its Jewish origins. Likewise, in our day we may in fact live to see a burgeoning faith as far removed from modern Christianity as first century Judaism was from the early church. You may question in yourself how this could be a good thing? Allow me to relate a story from the early days of my ministry:

In the late 1970's I mustered out of the Air Force where I served in Washington state during the days of the Carter administration and the Iran hostage crisis. My parents were pastoring a church in Lake Charles Louisiana and I made my home with them getting a job in a local grocery store handling produce. I was not close to the Lord at that time and in fact struggling against my childhood faith with great rebellion. I was haunted by the Scripture however that declares *"train up a child in the way should go and when he should go and when he is old will not depart from it…"* The fateful day came that I knelt at an altar and surrendered my life to Christ. In that commitment was kindled afresh and anew an open vision that came to me when I was 12 years old lying prostrate at the altar during a sawdust open air camp meeting. I saw the cross that was fixed to the pulpit of my home church in Clinton Missouri. It was a simple wooden cross adorning a plain, varnished pulpit in a dilapidated little Pentecostal church on the backside of town.

The Lord showed me that cross, rocking back and forth like a metronome and moving closer to me. As the metronome-cross moved closer, I noticed it did not sway back and forth quite as much – in fact when it was quite near to my field of vision it stood straight up and did not waver. I heard the voice of God speaking in the acoustics of my inner man: *"this represents your life for the next 12 years. You will waver and you will wonder but in the end you will stand for me."* The Lord went on to reveal to me that over those 12 years he would show me what it meant to take up my cross and follow Him. He then told me very clearly that at the conclusion of those 12 years of revealing the cross he would then begin for another, second 12 years time, to reveal the Throne. This was clearly a call to ministry that in my 12-year-old simplicity I accepted with fear and trembling. 11 years later I was given the opportunity to pastor my very first church.

The Sunday before my first sermon in this struggling little house church that met in my living room in Lake Charles Louisiana I was outside on the front porch pacing back and forth and praying. I simply wanted to survive the next 24 hours. I was terrified at the prospects of standing up and preaching a sermon to the small little group that had chosen to call me pastor. Typical to what I have learned in the years since, God did not speak to me about the immediacy of the next day's challenge. Instead he talked to me about things far into the future. As I paced back and forth in the sweltering late afternoon humidity, the Lord posed a question to me that I will repeat to you here:

"Is there any difference in character or tone between the religious system that crucified Jesus and modern day Christian culture?"

I have grown up in the church. My father was a pastor and my grandfather was a pastor. I had been in church almost every Sunday and Wednesday night for my entire life and attended many, many revivals that stretched sometimes for days on end. Even in my young adulthood I was well aware of the character and tone of the Christian religious system. The answer I gave to the voice of God rumbling in my heart was "Lord there is no difference between Christianity as I know it and what I read of the first century Judaism that crucified Jesus..." Then the Lord said something to me that I never forgot:

"I am coming to restore my people to my purpose, but I am not coming to restore the prevailing religious system that is Christianity as you know it".

He went on to say that in the first century it was according to plan when the prevailing religious system delivered Jesus over to the death of the cross. In the first coming of Jesus the substitutionary sacrifice had to be made. In the second coming of Christ however (the Lord said to me) He wasn't coming as a suffering Savior but as a reigning King. Whatever your eschatology may be or your belief regarding end time events, the intervening years between things as they are now and the millennial reign of Christ will be fleeting and brief. In the end, life will look much different for men on earth than it does now. You and I will live to see this great cosmic shift. Toward that end, I want to take a look with you through the lens of the prophetic anointing that God has placed on my life at the coming decades, in the hopes that we as fellow believers can place ourselves on the kingdom side of future history and not as many surely who will set themselves unwittingly in opposition against the emerging economy of God in our day.

Prophetic insight is one thing; scriptural precedent is another. Without indulging in some convoluted, formulaic, twisted timeline extracted from a fanciful imagination let us look to the words of the prophet Hosea for confirmation that we are living indeed at the crux of human history and in the threshold of the coming, millennial reign of Christ. In 2 Peter 3:8 the apostle Peter says this:

"but beloved be not ignorant of this one thing, that one day is with the Lord as 1000 years, and 1000 years as one day".

Taking that into consideration we can conclude that we are now living in the seventh 1000 year day of recorded history from the secularist point of view, and the seventh millennia from Adam, from the biblical worldview. The millennial reign is spoken of as "God's seventh day". With tongue firmly in cheek, let me predict a date for the Lord's return: at some point between the year 2000 (now past) and the year 3000 some 990 years in the future! The purpose of this writing is not to set a date for the Lord's return but rather to identify the season that we are now living in that you as an individual and we as a body might intelligently choose to be a part of the solution to what God is doing in the earth and not part of the problem. Let us read from an eschatological perspective the first three verses of Hosea chapter 6:

Hosea 6:1, and let us return to the Lord: for he has torn, and he will heal us; he has smitten, and he will bind is up. V. 2 after two days will he revive us: in the third day he will raise us up, and we shall live in his sight. V. 3 then shall we know, if we follow on to know the Lord: his going forth is prepared as the morning; and he shall come as the rain, as the latter and former rain unto the earth.

Calculating from the death, burial and resurrection of Jesus we are in the beginning of the third 1000 year day from the resurrection of Christ, and of the seventh 1000 year day from the garden of Eden. These two verses in Hosea, read from that point of view encapsulate in just a very few words the scope of human history since the time of Jesus. In the beginning of the first century mankind returned unto the Lord who had come and bled and died to establish His fledgling church on the day of Pentecost. Proceeding forward into the first millennium we find the outbreak of the bubonic plague and humanity and the church plunged into the tyranny of the dark ages when two out of every three men upon the earth particularly in Western Europe died of disease or were casualties of war (*he has torn*). As Hosea predicted we were torn in the first millennia from the resurrection. In the second millennium Hosea's prediction is "*he will heal us*". What happened in the second millennium after the resurrection of Jesus? In 1517 Martin Luther nailed his 99 theses onto the door of the Wittenberg Chapel and the Reformation was born and the simplicity of primitive faith in the Lord Jesus Christ was restored to mankind in a sweeping revival that registers still with missionary zeal among the nations of the earth.

In verse two the portended events looking forward from the close of the second millennia after the resurrection predict: "*after two days he will revive us*". When did the Reformation occur? In the second millennium after the resurrection of course. When did the Pentecostal outpouring in the Charismatic renewal take place? In the second millennium as we all know. We were torn and smitten in the first millennia after Christ and landed in the very depth of the dark ages. In the second millennia we were revived and experienced the Reformation, the Renaissance, the Great Awakening, the Industrial age, the Information age and the birth of the modern world as we now know it. What comes after the second day? We are now in the third 1000 year period of time after the resurrection of Jesus and the seventh 1000 year corresponding time measured from the expulsion of man from the garden of Eden. What does Hosea say then of this present "third day"?

Verse two says "in the third day he will raise us up, and we shall live in his sight". Let me say to you without any ambiguity – change is at hand! As the late John Wimber was wont to say *"God is asking us to relinquish church as we know it – for church as He wants it"*. The prevailing religious system (Judaism) of the first century was so entrenched in religious death they would rather crucify the Lord of glory then relinquish the tentacles of their ego and pride to the Lordship of their expected Messiah. What of the church of today? Unlike the Judaism of Jesus' day, the plan of God will not be thwarted. There will be no suffering Messiah. It will be God's way or no way as He raises up a people who will live in his sight and follow on to know Him as He is known in a true outpouring and fulfillment of the rain, the latter and a former rain of God's Spirit poured out in a single season of time in the beginning of the third millennia that we are now living in.

The question for you and I is: *are we going to follow on to know the Lord?* Or are we going to cling to the familiar? Are you going to follow the anointing or remain ensconced in the brick and masonry mausoleums of an anemic religious culture incapable of knowing the day of their visitation even as Jerusalem, scant years before the destruction of Temple?

CHAPTER 3
AFRICAN AMERICAN PROMOTION CONTINUES

The message of the gospel is good news not just to individuals but to people groups and specifically, *ethnicities*. When you use this word it often leads to a minefield of political correctness and misconceptions. We will ignore all of these shallow considerations and give what God has impressed us with for the benefit of the disenfranchised people groups of the earth – specifically in this chapter the African-American demographic. If you are an African-American, you are living in pivotal times. There was never a season in the earth when the assault of the enemy AND the promise of God is coming into great juxtaposition and contrast. This is promotion time for you. Be not afraid. Embrace your destiny as an African-American for God's hand is adjudicating in behalf of your race to rectify centuries old injustices. You will see it clearly and in fact it has already begun.

God works in a time frame of history. This year is the 500th year that persons of African descent have been exploited on the North American continent. When Columbus navigated to the Western hemisphere, the Nina was piloted by an African sailor, and a slave served as Columbus' cabin boy. The little known fact is, that Columbus was the initiator and father of African slavery as we have known it in the last many centuries of history. When Columbus came to the Americas, he hoped to exploit the natives (Incas and Mayans) by bringing them to western Africa as slaves. They proved to be inadaptable to slave labor. Failing this Columbus turned to African slaves and the slave trade that bolstered the economies of the Renaissance was born. Long before the first Native American laid eyes on a white man African slaves were the stock and trade of the European nations whose enforced labor was an indispensable component of the development of the western world. By 1867 more than 12.7 million men, women and children of African descent had been sold on the auction blocks of North America and the United States. Viewed from a scope of many centuries, the social debt incurred by the west upon African peoples is starkly apparent.

After 500 years of slavery and disenfranchisement, God's hand is sovereignly promoting those of African descent to the highest echelons of power and accomplishment across every field of endeavor. As a person of African extraction you are poised for promotion and blessing more than you could ever realize. This is the good news to the African nations (or *ethnos*).

One of the core values of the kingdom of God and our heavenly Father is His inalienable sense of justice. The Father is committed to a campaign of Ethnic Justice in the earth. What religion cannot fix and what politics cannot fix, God is moving - to right the scales of Ethnic Justice in behalf of the minority people groups in the earth and the African-American people will be among the primary beneficiaries of that program of God. God has heard the groanings of the African peoples of the earth. As He heard the cry of His people under Pharaoh and sent deliverance God likewise has heard the cry of the African-American people and is answering in His sovereignty.

In Matt. 28:19 and Mark 13:10, Jesus stated that the gospel is the Gospel to the nations. That word NATIONS is the word ETHNOS from which we also derive the word ETHNICITY. It is a fundamental truth that the gospel is a gospel of salvation from injustice, from bondage, from exploitation and where that has existed, God will right the balances, working from an economy of scale spanning not just decades but centuries. God works not only on an individual level to bring the claims of Christ to bear upon the individual but He also works on the scope of whole ethnicities to bring out His justice and His purpose. If you are a minority this is cause for rejoicing. If you are member of the majority this thought might give you pause. Regardless of how you receive it the purpose of God is clear – for the African peoples the Spirit of God has declared in the earth that though they were *FIRST IN SUFFERING they will now be FIRST IN PROMOTION*. This is so obvious when you answer the question why would God put an African-American in the Oval Office before a Hispanic or a white woman? A Hispanic or white woman would be infinitely more electable but God is in control. Am I suggesting that God put Barack Obama in office? I am not only suggesting it I am declaring it and will give scriptural precept to back it up.

In ancient Israel there was a famine that would not lift in King David's time. When consulting the prophets and the Urim and Thummim it was discovered that an ethnic injustice from long before required correction, in order to bring God's blessing on the land again:

> *[2Sa 21:1-3 KJV] 1 Then there was a famine in the days of David three years, year after year; and David enquired of the LORD. And the LORD answered, [It is] for Saul, and for [his] bloody house, because he slew the Gibeonites. 2 And the king called the Gibeonites, and said unto them; (now the Gibeonites [were] not of the children of Israel, but of the remnant of the Amorites; and the children of Israel had sworn unto them: and Saul sought to slay them in his*

zeal to the children of Israel and Judah.) 3 Wherefore David said unto the Gibeonites, What shall I do for you? and wherewith shall I make the atonement, that ye may bless the inheritance of the LORD?

Again, it has been said that God moves in 500 year strides through history. This can be described as God's linear purpose through time. There were approximately 500 years between the writing of the book of Malachi and the coming of Jesus and establishment of the early church. There were 500 years from the crucifixion of Jesus to the fall of the Roman empire. 500 years later the schism between the Eastern Orthodox Church and the Western Roman church was formalized, laying the foundation for the cultural divide between east and west in the modern world. 500 years later Martin Luther came on the scene at the same time Columbus opens the New World to Christianity. 500 years later, a man of African descent becomes the leader of the free world and of the most powerful nation on the earth. As of the writing of this chapter we not only see African-Americans rising to power in the political arena, but in other endeavors as well, such as media pundit Brian Williams being usurped by the hand of God and Lester Holt – an African-American taking his place. There are many other examples and they will be in abundance in days to come.

How would God go about putting a president in office? Don't the voters decide who leads a representative government? Beyond the scope of President Obama's ideology, beyond the political intrigues of the right or the left, conservative or liberal, President Obama's election signals the fullness of time in God's campaign of ethnic justice in behalf of all peoples of African descent in the western world and African-American people in particular. To those who resent President Obama's election I refer you to the following scripture:

[Dan 2:20-21 KJV Blessed be the name of God for ever and ever... he removeth kings, and setteth up kings...

To reiterate, Proverbs 16:33 tells us that man may cast a lot but God decides the outcome. Man may pull the voting lever but God holds the key to the executive washroom in the Oval Office. If you reject the leader of our nation you reject the sovereignty of God. The scriptures plainly and undeniably assert that His hand controls the outcome of elections, etc. Regardless of the outcome of an election if we believe the scriptures we can only acquiesce to the sovereignty of God who determines with finality, who rules our nations and the nations of the earth. To dispute this is to question the clear testimony of God's holy word. Does this mean we accept everything our leaders do or say? No it does not. But understand this – you are not the first believer to live under a hostile regime. The early church suffered deeply under governments and leaders whose character dwarfs in their magnitude the worst examples of despotism today. Nonetheless the early church was NOT an insurgent church nor was it a activist (political) church. Yet in three hundred years they brought the known world to its knees at the foot of the cross. How did this happen? *By how they prayed and how they died.* In the midst of brutal persecution and geopolitical chaos what was the counsel of the apostles and early church fathers?

The apostle Paul commanded us:

[1Ti 2:1-3 KJV] 1 I exhort therefore, that, first of all, supplications, prayers, intercessions, [and] giving of thanks, be made for all men; 2 For kings, and [for] all that are in authority; that we may lead a quiet and peaceable life in all godliness and honesty. 3 For this [is] good and acceptable in the sight of God our Saviour;

To those who have rejected President Obama and fantasized about the military overthrow of the federal government, or the assassination of our president I submit to you that your problem is not a political problem or a Democrat problem but a God problem. For 60 years the conservative party has dominated the executive branch of Government and they have largely done so by coopting the theme of "God and Country". The Republican Party has seduced the church and convinced Christians to exchange the altar of prayer for political power and manipulation. This has failed miserably for almost 30 years yet the beat goes on for "four more years" and "all will be well".

The church of the living God has thus been reduced to the profane status of becoming a marginalized Washington lobbying group. The Republican party has manipulated the Christian electorate by blaming the Democrats for all the social ills in our society while they themselves have not delivered on ONE ITEM of the Christian political agenda from the inception of the Moral Majority under Jerry Falwell right down to today. Instead conservative politicos vilify the Democratic party and claim the only answer is "Four more years…" Because of this and because they have denigrated the people of God, and the name of Christ to a mere political tool – the Father says that the *BISHOP'S PRICK, THE BISHOP'S STAFF of the executive branch of government has been taken from the conservative right and given to the political left for the next fifty years.* Do not be blinded by political ideology to the higher purposes of God. The Father put Barack Obama in office in pursuit of a higher purpose of ethnic justice that far exceeds in its scope and influence the effect of the Obama administration on the affairs of the country. Learn to see past the ground cover of the political and see the spiritual geography of the kingdom being established in behalf (in this case) of the African American peoples. President Obama is only the beginning. Brian Williams being replaced by Lester Holt is only the beginning. The time of promotion is at hand for those of African descent – your time is now.

You may look at now the second term of President Obama's tenure and think that this time is coming to an end. This is not the ending of something but the beginning of something. The tenure of President Obama has been like a birth canal to birth God's purpose in the African-American people. Who would have thought that the term of an African-American president would be marked by the worst season of race relations in the United States since Martin Luther King? The enemy is raging war on the vulnerable youth of the African-American people in the United States. He knows his time is short and he is raging both in the police state and in the lowest elements of the black race to abort the time of promotion and blessing that is upon this disenfranchised people. Just as Herod came against the children of promise so as with the Travon Martin case (and many others) African-American young people have not been as vulnerable as they are today since the 60's and 70's. But God's purpose will not be denied.

The word of God over the African American people is:

First in Suffering – First in Promotion.

From this time forward you are going to see African-American men and women moving to the forefront of every major field of endeavor in western culture. Not just in sports, but in Finance, Business, Government, the Military, Entertainment, Medicine, Education and the Arts and Religion as well. African-American men and women will not just be the beneficiaries of the bounty of these realms but they will increasingly be the decision makers, and the movers and shakers across every strata of western society as God rights the scales of ethnic justice in their behalf. At the time of this writing we had only Barack Obama to point to but now many other prominent black achievers are coming to the forefront as media giants, barons of industry, powerful legislators and many other positions of power. This is only the beginning of what God is doing and we should rejoice as He adjudicates in the earth for the black race against 500 years of injustice.

First in Suffering – First in Promotion.

It is not by mere chance that an African-American man is the first minority to sit in the oval office. Before a woman, or a Hispanic or other minority God used an African-American to go before and break through in behalf of other people groups. In the next ten election cycles you will see a Hispanic man and an Anglo woman in the White-house, but the forerunner in this and every major field of endeavor for the next half-century will be African-American men and women, chosen not by man or by the church but by the Father because He is God and He can do anything He wants any time He wants and He doesn't have to check with anybody.

Two Anglo Prophets – God's chosen messengers:

God didn't choose to deliver this message through a minority ministry but through two Anglo-Americans (myself and my spouse Kitty). You see when David summoned the Gibeonites, he knew the famine wouldn't lift until the Gibeonites blessed their former oppressors in the name of the Lord. Therefore, God sent two white prophets with this message in order that the cultural divide between black and white would be closed by an act of humility through two unsung, unknown prophetic servants. The response called for from the African-American community is one of embrace of the message and forgiveness of those who have personally, socially and institutionally oppressed them.

The Father told us in 2009 that we would prophesy to "people groups and people groups and people groups". This includes African-Americans, Hispanics, and Anglos. In 2012 Dr. Rosalys Martinez invited us to speak to a conference of Hispanic churches and to bring "the prophetic word to the Hispanic People". This was the beginning of the fulfillment of the prophecy in 2009 whereby we have prophesied to audience of up to 30 million Hispanic believers on televsion. This conference was held in the church home of an African-American congregation. The pastor came up afterwards and asked "when are you going to prophesy to OUR PEOPLE". Just as Dr. Martinez asked for the Hispanic people and that word was delivered so when this pastor asked, there came an answer. When you ask the prophet it will be God that answers. When you can't ask your prophet because you don't want him or her to speak about something, you inform them about - then you don't want a prophet you want a psychic. But God sent two Anglo prophets to bring the gospel of Ethnic Justice to the Hispanics, likewise He sent us to the African-American people with this GOOD NEWS.

The Gibeonites were a slave people. God cares for the disenfranchised of the earth. Whether man cooperates or not – God is sovereign. The cries you have cried out with for your children and your children's children are being answered. You might ask what about the return of Christ. Jesus said "occupy till I come…." Expect him to come tomorrow but work and plan like He isn't coming for a 1000 years. I have news for you, that is how God himself conducts His business. Go ahead and dream. *Go ahead and plan says the Father for I am with you both to will and to do My good pleasure.*

CHAPTER 4
A COMING HISPANIC MAJORITY

In 2012 my wife Kitty and I gave up our home, gave away or sold all our possessions and went into the nation to teach, preach and prophesy. During this time, we preached in 66 cities in the US living totally on the road. We traveled to six countries soon after. Early on in this assignment we received a call from Dr. Rosalys Martinez. She asked us to come to a conference of Hispanic churches in West Palm Beach and "to bring the "Impartation of God for the Hispanic community in 2013."

When praying about this meeting the Father spoke this to my heart:

The Hispanic community in the United States is coming to promotion. The Father is bringing His purposes in the Hispanic community to a tipping point in the year 2013 and the years beyond.

This request was the first fulfillment of the prophetic word given to us in 2009 that we would prophesy to "people groups and people groups and people groups…" It was interesting that a Hispanic person would reach out to us in this way because when God gave us the assignment to go into the nation, He told us that the time would come that we would have an indefinite assignment to minister in a Hispanic country. Neither Kitty nor myself speak Spanish nor had we any meaningful interaction with Hispanic people up to this point. So the invitation was very telling and had all the earmarks of a "God thing" that we embraced wholeheartedly.

When God gave us the word of the Lord for the Hispanic conference I asked Him why this was going to happen. The Father said *"there is an innate humility in the Hispanic people that has moved My hand to respond and bring them to greatness in the earth and specifically in the United States."*

The scripture reference came to me found in the first letter of Peter:

> *1Pe 5:6 KJV - Humble yourselves therefore under the mighty hand of God, that he may exalt you in due time:*

Those in whom humility is found will find themselves thrust into the DUE TIME of God's mighty hand.

> *Jam 4:6 KJV - But he giveth more grace. Wherefore he saith, God resisteth the proud, but giveth grace unto the humble.*

Even members of other oppressed minorities often readily acknowledge the admirable work ethic and humility of the Hispanic peoples. God resists (sets his forces in array - against the proud) but gives grace (His empowering presence) to the humble. The scripture cannot be broken. The Hispanic people come to this country and take jobs no one else will work at and humble themselves as servants in our society. By biblical principle it is inevitable that they as a people come to majority and come to promotion. We will see this in our lifetime. The Anglo demographic in the US will one day be replaced as the predominant ethnicity in the US by the Hispanic population.

The invitation of the King of Kings to the Hispanic community is reflected in the words of Jesus in the gospel of Luke:

> *Luk 14:10 KJV - But when thou art bidden, go and sit down in the lowest room; that when he that bade thee cometh, he may say unto thee, Friend, go up higher:*

Why is this going to happen? Because God has an autonomic response to humility. You as a Hispanic have occupied the low place. You have been despised and used and looked upon as a commodity to be exploited. But the Father says:

> *Isa 57:15 KJV - For thus saith the high and lofty One that inhabiteth eternity, whose name [is] Holy; I dwell in the high and holy [place], with him also [that is] of a contrite and humble spirit, to revive the spirit of the humble, and to revive the heart of the contrite ones.*

In Zech. 2:8 the Father said that you are as the apple (or pupil) of His eye. When someone touches you or puts his finger in your eye you have an automatic response to defend yourself. Likewise, when the Father finds humility in your heart, His autonomic response is to **DEFEND, PROTECT, PRESERVE AND PROMOTE YOU**. The word **HUMILITY** in the bible means to **GO LOW**. Have you ever watched the weather on TV and noticed that the rain clouds always gather to the **LOW** place in the atmosphere? Jesus said the kingdom works just this way:

> *Mat 16:3 KJV - And in the morning, [It will be] foul weather to day: for the sky is red and lowring. O [ye] hypocrites, ye can discern the face of the sky; but can ye not [discern] the signs of the times?*

Jesus is saying to us that by learning about how our weather system works, we learn how the kingdom works. There are seven great jet streams of wind that circle the earth creating our weather.

Meteorologists will tell you that when those winds encounter a low pressure area they will pour out of their beneficial rains in that area.

Likewise, just as there are seven natural winds that bring the beneficial rains to the LOW places of the earth – even so Isa. 11:1-3 says that there are SEVEN SPIRITS OF GOD that respond to those who are GOING LOW and walking in humility (in this case the Hispanic people). When the Father finds humility in your life or in a people the seven spirits of God bend low and pour out the rains of the Holy Spirit upon that people to bring them to their destiny.

What are the seven Spirits of God? Isa. 11:1-3 tells us they are the Spirit of the Lord, the Spirit of Wisdom, Understanding, Counsel, Might, Knowledge and the Fear of the Lord. God begins with the Spirit of the Fear of the Lord and causes us to ascend in worship to the knowledge, might, counsel, understanding, wisdom and finally the Spirit of the Lord Himself activated over you as a people to bring you to your destiny. These are even as the rungs of the ladder that Jacob saw at Bethel in the night when he was fleeing from Esau.

Luk 19:26 KJV - For I say unto you, That unto every one which hath shall be given; and from him that hath not, even that he hath shall be taken away from him.

God is taking the bishop's staff of leadership in this country and majority rule from that people who have proven themselves unworthy of it and passing it on to the Hispanic community and the African American community because the Father has found an innate humility in the Hispanic people He can work with to bring His glory.

Observations and Conclusion: The Pew Research Foundation states that in recent years the Hispanic community has exploded in growth to being the second largest people group in the US. Census data and Pew's research indicate that at the current rate of growth the Hispanic community will become THE MAJORITY ethnicity in the United States in slightly less than one generation.

I asked the Father what this meant. He said that within three election cycles the Hispanic community will have the opportunity not only to determine who sits in the White House but to place a Hispanic leader in the Oval Office. This man will be a conservative but his loyalties will be to his God before any political ideology or creed.

The bishop's staff of growth, blessing and leadership is passing from its existing hands to the Hispanic community and African American community in the United States and your eyes will see it and you will reap the rewards as you align yourselves with God's revealed purposes in the next season.

CHAPTER 5
24 COMING EVENTS

While attending a local meeting with apostle Warren Hunter I was caught up in the Spirit and was given a list of 24 things that will befall the world in the next 50 years. Each item was given in my spirit in a concise and unambiguous way which I will attempt to convey here. Initially, I only had my iPhone to take notes with so the list was rather terse as reflects the style of typing that is done on the keypad of a phone. After reproducing that list here, I will enlarge upon this list and clarify it in subsequent chapters:

One: As stated previously, the place of leadership in the US dominated by the RNC will be radically changed. For the next many decades the RNC will not overshadow the Oval Office as in recent years.

Two: A liberal woman, a member of the DNC will come to power as President of the United States. She will be raised up by the sovereignty of God and pull the country back from the brink of economic disaster.

Three: A homosexual president will sit in the Oval Office. The DNC will capitalize on the political cache of this woman president and succeed in nominating and electing in a general election a homosexual man to the presidency of the United States.

Four: The church will experience a great disillusionment. In the aftermath of political disaster, the church, particularly the Evangelical churches will term these events as "The Great Disillusionment".

Five: An unprecedented prayer initiative will follow. After many decades of misdirection, the Evangelical church will once again turn to a massive prayer movement such as has not been seen since the early centuries of the church.

Six: A great awakening will emerge. Out of this prayer initiative an expected move of God will come that many will not understand or support. A new generation of young people with great missionary zeal will emerge, but they will not be advocates of what they will term "the Establishment church" which they will reject, including the Pentecostal/Charismatic stream in all its forms.

Seven: A new Evangelical movement will be born. Out of this grass roots outpouring a new Evangelical movement will coalesce which will encapsulate a great emphasis on the new birth experience in a very organic and holistic way. Over just a few decades this movement will define the purposes of God in the earth and every church organization outside this movement, or failing to embrace it will become the new nominalism or "Christian in name only".

Eight: Young Arabic apostles will come. Out of the Arabian Peninsula will emerge 8 young Arabic apostles from the ranks of Jihadist radicalism.

Nine: Ethnic justice will be executed. The Hispanic, African, and First Nations Peoples of North America and Western Europe will rise to ascendancy in business, the economy, politics as well as social, and cultural arenas. The impoverishment and marginalization of these people groups will be greatly ameliorated by the hand of God who has determined "enough is enough".

Ten: The Union will come under great stress and cessation of many states will be threatened. The economic and social pressures in the United States will fuel a great upsurge of cessationist sentiment and many states will seriously and widely ponder withdrawing from the union. National Guard units and Federal troops will have minor clashes that will be trivialized in the media in hopes of maintaining order and the cohesiveness of the national integrity of our borders and our nation.

Eleven: A great natural disaster will strike the Midwest followed by the eruption of the Yellowstone caldera. Volcanic activity at Yellowstone will increase dramatically with a large eruption that will disrupt air travel and the commerce of the state of Wyoming and surrounding states as well. Yellowstone as a viable and desired tourist destination will be greatly curtailed as public sentiment embraces the apocalyptic vision of a worst-case scenario regarding Yellowstone volcanic activity.

Twelve: A land invasion of the U.S. will be thrown back by a weakened military. There will be a new axis of power influenced by Iran, China and North Korea. It will be a border incident that will affect the United States as deeply as the 911 attacks and shape American politics for many years.

Thirteen: The UK and Southern Europe will see a great revival. The revival that will break out on the east coast of the United States will make itself known in the United Kingdom and specifically southern Europe.

Fourteen: Africa will pay its love debt to the United Kingdom. The Christianization of Africa will spill over in a great Missionary initiative by African immigrants that will measurably reestablish the New Evangelical Movement in that part of the world.

Fifteen: The Hispanic people and other minorities will usurp white privilege. Over the next fifty years the Hispanic minority will become the majority ethnicity in North America and in 100 years they will be the dominant people group of the Western World.

Sixteen: Out of the African races will come a new elite. In every field of endeavor African peoples will distinguish themselves in medicine, business, the halls of academia and in the service of the military in many western countries.

Seventeen: Out of the white races a spiritual nation of servant sons will come. There will be established a major seat of learning once again in Northern Ireland. Belfast and Northern Ireland will again become a center of learning and academic excellence. Many advances in medicine and science will be pioneered by practitioners, researchers and mathematicians and theorists from these centers.

Eighteen: The UK the U.S., and France will be brought to its knees at the foot of the cross. Revival will sweep across the UK, the USA and France in a radical way. Secularism will be defeated in France and a new zeal of the Lord's house will emerge on the streets of Paris.

Nineteen: Islam will be marginalized by internal strife and civil war. The Islamists will become so occupied with warring against each other that their campaigns against the west will be greatly diminished.

Twenty: The U.S. and Russia will become a petro-center in the modern economy. A new western energy oligarchy will emerge as an economic superpower. Fracking technologies and massive new discoveries of natural gas will be found in North America and Europe. The West will move into energy independence and the petro-balance of the world will shift away from the unstable Middle East.

Twenty-One: Helsinki, Finland will become an enclave of prophetic ministry supporting a missions initiative in northern Europe. The spiritual heritage of northern Europe will be restored. Suicide rates in Finland and northern Europe will be reduced to statistical zero because of the outpouring of the Spirit of God in that part of the world.

Twenty-Two: Antarctica will become an international Guantanamo where the nations of the West will warehouse terrorists and international criminals. In fact, the Father says that it already is – but it is being kept secret. Those things done in secret will be revealed.

Twenty-Three: A Republican senator will be assassinated and a presidential election will be shifted in the ensuing events.

Twenty-Four: The spouse of this slain legislator will be the first woman conservative to take the White House.

This list will be reproduced in further detail in another form and version elsewhere in these chapters. What must we make of such predictions? God did not give me these things to generate alarm or dismay among His people. I am absolutely convinced in my heart that the "sky isn't falling the kingdom is coming". It is irresponsible on any person's part to sound an alarm without pointing to hope. It doesn't take any prophetic gifting to predict doom and gloom. God is not a doom and gloom God. Yet we live in a fallen world and as the saying goes, "stuff happens". If we will listen God will speak to us. It is not the intention of heaven that these things come upon us unawares. Throughout history some of the most robust seasons of church growth and strength have been in times of tremendous social upheaval. Know that God is with us. Know that He will never leave us or forsake us.

Where do our dependencies and security lie? With the solidarity of the Union? Then in the United States if that be the case we are already in deep trouble. The fissures of the social divide in this country are widening by the day. Men and woman of faith are being marginalized, and in fact tossed aside by a population that is increasingly non-Christian if not anti-Christian. We live, brothers and sisters in a post-Christian society and in a country that now only in name can say "in God we trust". Is that a terrible thing? For those who reject Christ yes. For those of us who have entrusted our lives to the Lordship of Jesus Christ we realize that God is with us regardless what regime or government we are made subject to. Our trust is in the Lord not in democracy. Our trust is in the God of Abraham, Isaac and Jacob not in the noble experiment of representative government that is these United States.

All forms of government have a life cycle. You need only look back at the last 20 years and see the pressures bursting our form of government at its seams. The executive is largely powerless, the legislature is impotent and the judicial branch is increasingly showing itself to be completely out of touch with the mainstream of our population. Some see in this, a deep conspiracy but in reality it is simply the advanced middle-age of our form of government teetering toward its natural end. Any government historically that gives itself over to giving unchecked entitlements to its people is nearing its end. The decay of Ancient Rome for instance can be measured in the picture of Praetorians meeting the advancing mob and throwing bread to the starving people. That only works for a while. The need and demand of the people always outstrips the capacity of government to supply. Then the end comes. It isn't the end of the world – just the end of a way of life. Christianity predates democracy and will survive past it's end. The sky isn't falling the kingdom is coming.

Can the things listed in these 24 predictions be avoided? If they don't come to pass does that make me a false prophet? Jesus prophesied that the 12 disciples would sit on thrones judging Israel. Judas was among them and his disobedience rendered this prediction by Jesus inaccurate. Does this make Jesus a false prophet? Do we judge the prophecy by the rebellious spirit of the people or the rebellious spirit of the people by the prophesy? Jonah predicted the destruction of Nineveh – but nothing happened. Does this make Jonah a false prophet? Hardly. All prophecy is provisional and conditional. I believe one reason prophesies are given at this level is so people will pray and thereby what is prophesied (as in Jonah's case) can be averted. Alarmists, and spiritual pugilists may scoff but the nuance and reality of how the prophetic works in regard to fulfillment cannot be ignored or impeached by inane, backward thinking, small minded, Pygmalion religious mentalities. Put your faith in God. Pray out the things you read in this book. Let God lead and direct your responses to determine what it means to you personally. The end result for you will be benefit and blessing.

CHAPTER 6
A NEW GREAT AWAKENING!

There is going to be a Great Awakening in our time. This has been prophesied around the world and it has been prophesied here for decades by many well-known and respected ministers and ministries. God is calling His men and women around the world to speak into this vision and pray into this vision and to curate this vision that God has already established. There is going to be a Great Awakening in our time. It will come forth in the aftermath of a Great Disillusionment for the church. As a result, God's people will begin to pray with an intensity not seen since the early centuries of the church. In answer to this God will send a new Great Awakening. It will begin on the east coast of the US, and soon spread around the world. God is now calling up intercessors and spiritual moms and dads to have the spirit of a mid-wife to give birth to this thing that He is doing.

The coming Great Awakening will begin in the younger generations. The church will not initially accept this new cohort of mission minded young people. They will be orphaned from the establishment church but will find their spiritual DNA in a contingent of servant minded mothers and fathers who will validate their zeal and passion for Christ. Affirmed by their spiritual mentors, these young lions without religious pedigree will burst on the world scene with great fervor to confront the nations of the earth with the claims of Christ.

Just as the Evangelical movement was birthed from the Great Awakening in the 1700's a new Evangelical movement will come forth from this awakening to redefine faith, church and Christian culture. The establishment church will become marginalized in the light of a new generation of radical Jesus loving believers.

"It's a new day", says the Father and the invitation is extended to prepare to receive this generation He is raising up – to affirm and validate them as they pour their lives out like drink offerings to King Jesus. Toward that end we are laboring because we believe and many prophets and seers before us have confirmed that Branson Missouri will have her portion in a great outpouring of God's Spirit. We cannot make it happen but we can stand in testament and speak into this vision and lean into it with our prayers and our intercession. Likewise, you in your part of the world must tap into and pray into the vision of a global outpouring as it connects to your community, region and nation.

This is a call to prayer and to prepare as apostolic mothers and fathers to receive this dynamic generation that the Lord is sending. In every enclave of hungry believers God is extending an overture of this revival – foreseen by many gospel luminaries over the years. In a time of prayer God spoke this to me *"Branson Missouri will have its moment as the Evangelical Center of the Earth"* (8 years on God's timetable [2 Pet. 3:8]). Your community, your city, your church is no different. Reach out for this. Pray into this. Make it your passion and your determination to be a participator and a first partaker of what God is doing in this hour.

What was the Great Awakening? In the 1700's during a time known as the Enlightenment or the Age of Reason a movement swept America that became known as the Great Awakening. It changed the way people thought about God and how they thought about themselves. It eventually came to define Christianity, as we know it. The Great Awakening engaged the hearts of the people with an emotionally charged gospel of redemption and individual accountability to the Lordship of Jesus.

The Great Awakening focused on spiritual transformation, personal decision and dedication to Christ. The whole idea of "making a decision for Christ" was at the forefront of the Great Awakening. Before the Great Awakening the "altar call" was unknown in western Christianity. The New Birth suddenly became a matter of a personal encounter with Christ. Institutional religion was only valid after the Great Awakening insofar as it facilitated the spread of the gospel regarding personal salvation and the new birth. Missions were strongly emphasized and in time, out of the Great Awakening was birthed a phenomena known as the Evangelical Movement. Soon the Evangelical movement consolidated into various organizations and denominations. Everything outside its influence became marginalized and rendered ineffective. It came to be that Christianity outside of the Evangelical movement - - didn't matter.

Who were the carriers of the glory of the Great Awakening? George Whitefield and Jonathan Edwards were prominent ministers in the Great Awakening. Their goal was to get their listeners to have a personal, emotional response to the message of Christ. They wanted their hearers to look into their own souls and become convinced of their need of a savior.

Jonathan Edwards is often credited with starting the Great Awakening in 1741 with his famous sermon "Sinners in the Hands of an Angry God".

Imagine this. One day. One gathering. One singular response of the people and all of human history pivots away from secularism and rejection of Christ into a movement that entirely changed the parameters of what it meant to be a believer and what Christianity would look like in the earth.

Regarding the Great Awakening and its meetings: Jonathan Edwards encouraged people to come "not just for curiosity but from a sincere desire to know God and do your duty as a believer in Christ." Mere curiosity and religious titillation was considered to be the hallmark of a lukewarm heart. He urged people not to apply the mandates of Christ to others (as the Puritans and Quakers were known to do) but to look into their hearts and ask 'Lord is it I?'

George Whitefield taught people to have changed and repentant hearts. In the Western world Whitefield is credited with starting the practice of preaching in public because the organized churches in England would not give him a pulpit. Whitefield responded to the rejection of institutional religion by obeying God and taking the message from those that were initially invited, out into the highways and by-ways where he found willing listeners.

Another well-known speaker by the name of James Davenport held public bonfires so his followers could burn the things that distracted them from kingdom seeking or tempted them to worldliness and pride. Non-religious books and luxury items were commonly cast into the flames. One night he derided the cult of celebrity and the idolatry of fashion and "fancy clothes". Leading by example to the shock of the crowd he took off his pants and threw them into the fire!

These were men and women willing to push the envelope of acceptability. They would not take no for an answer. The legacy of the Great Awakening was to push the boundaries of Spiritual propriety outside the realm of tradition and religion. They took matters of faith out of the ghetto of religion and walked in the kingdom in the spheres of business, education, government, etc. The resulting reforms changed the way business was done, government was conducted and ultimately even slavery was ended and many other social ills of the day were addressed.

There are generations of people and specific leaders that shape culture and change history: John Wimber, founder of the Vineyard movement made the statement before his death:

God is asking us to relinquish church as we know it for church as God wants it. Things are the way they are because of what WE are doing.

If WE want something different we must DO something different. We cannot look to the world and lament how dark and how godless it is. We must look at ourselves and lament that we have become so powerless and such a laughingstock in the earth that the fear of God is no longer known among men as once it was. In generations past the world trembled before the church and our leaders confronted nations. There came a day in the third century that world powers dared to no longer mock the Christ of Christianity, in spite of centuries of persecution. In the third century we have an example of a church that in three generations brought the known world to its knees at the foot of the cross. The might of Rome was so bowed to the power of God that its emperor faced the fact that the future of the Roman Empire could only advance under the sign of the cross.

The early church was neither an activist church nor an insurgent church. It didn't not take up arms or attempt to bring change through the legislative processes available to it. The church of the first, second and third centuries is remarkable for two things: *The way they prayed; and; The way the died.*

The Roman procurators who oversaw the martyrdoms of the early church complained to the emperor. They insisted that the Christians died so well that for every believer killed in the arena 100 were taking their place. The early church was not seen as a religion. In fact, the ancient world when confronted with "those that have turned the world upside down" didn't know how to deal with them. Most early Christians were not martyred for what they believed. but were rather condemned and sentenced as atheists.

> *This generation of believers defied definition. They didn't fit. They challenged the status quo and intimidated every ancient institution with their zeal and passion for Jesus.*

A radical commitment to the gospel:

> *There is rising again such a generation in the earth. There is coming a generation of believers who will sell their lives cheap for the cause of Christ. As the Moravians of old their watchword will be "may the lamb receive the reward of His suffering. Jihadist extremism will pale before the burning love for God this generation will exemplify. They will confront nations and the media will be unable to ignore them. The church will be unable to marginalize them. Young people will go into the mission field with nothing but a passport and a bible and will willingly sacrifice their lives for the cause of Christ.*

Again, this Great Awakening will be known for two things - the way they pray and the way they die. Martyrdoms will surge to a level that hasn't been seen since the days of the early church. They will pray on a scale that hasn't been seen since the days that Paul was writing the New Testament. What about the establishment church? On the east coast this revival will break out led by unlikely young people out of the rural areas of Pennsylvania and the Appalachians. Governors and city leaders will convene to consider what response is necessary to quell a movement they don't understand. This Great Awakening generation will have a COMPLETE disconnect from what they will term "THE ESTABLISHMENT CHURCH". The establishment church will reject this movement though its ranks will be filled with their own children. This movement will not initially accept full gospel, Charismatic, or Pentecostal doctrine or practice. They will identify these influences as part of the establishment church and reject them completely.

Let it be known that this Great Awakening *will not validate the Pentecostal, Charismatic, Full Gospel demographic in the modern church.* BUT, if Spirit filled Christians will reach out to this generation and love them and accept them and give them the affirmation denied them - then they will accept the baptism of the Holy Ghost, Signs, Wonders, and the Gifts of the Spirit. When this happens there will be a detonation of revival outpouring that will challenge the world on a scale unprecedented in modern times.

Examples from our times: Do we have any modern examples of this kind of movement? Fuller Theological Seminary claims that the Jesus Movement of the 1960's and 70's actually brought more people to Christ than the Great Awakening did. The Jesus Movement was an orphaned outpouring. Even in the churches where it was tolerated the environment was toxic to the revival. Kids were rejected because of the way they dressed, how they talked, the way they smelled - by a powerless church that didn't come close to having the effectiveness that this rowdy, unkempt, unruly generation did in bringing millions to Christ.

How will the next Great Awakening come? There is coming ahead for the church in America and the church in the Western World what will be called "the Great Disillusionment". The establishment church in America is about to be disenfranchised in the political arena in such a way that their political aspirations will be publicly and openly crushed. As a result, they will turn from these dependencies and begin to pray on an unprecedented scale. They will cry out to God as they did in the Great Depression and in answer to prayer God will send this Outpouring. He will answer their prayer but they will not understand the answer He sends. As a result, the establishment church will become a part of the problem rather than a part of the solution.

The Great Awakening in Western Europe: In spite of the lack of endorsement from established churches and groups this movement will ignite, in the city of London and in Northern England and Northern Ireland. Africa will pay its love debt to the United Kingdom for its missionary efforts on the dark continent during the days of when the sun never set on the British Empire.

What is your part? Are you willing to be an advance worker in this outpouring? Are you willing to place yourself in advance of this outpouring as Father David Nash did in advance of Charles Finney's revivals? Nash would go ahead of Finney a year ahead of time to pray for revival and when Finney showed up people would run out of their homes begging for repentance and whole communities were transformed. When Nash retired Finney quit preaching revival because the power was gone. Are you willing to be a part? Are you willing to pray into this? Or are you going to sit back and observe with a wait and see attitude - to which posture the KINGDOM WILL NEVER COME.

What about Branson, Missouri? Branson is dear to our heart because it is home to our ministry. God spoke to me in prayer saying "Branson Missouri will have its moment as the Evangelical Center of the Earth". Do we have examples of this? Are there cities that were ground zero for what became spiritual movements with a much broader context? Think Azusa Street, Pensacola, New Hebrides, the Welsh Revival under Evan Roberts, and others too numerous to mention.

Since coming here, we have connected with several other men and women of God who were led to Branson at about the same time. Apostle Don Matison, Prophet Jess Bielby, others to be sure. They didn't come here with any financial backing or promise of gain. They came at their own expense, selling themselves into what they perceived by the Spirit was a great thing about to happen in this city.

Where does Branson come in and why would God be interested in doing anything in the Ozarks of Missouri? There are fewer than 10,000 permanent residents here yet millions of people come here every year as tourists. Branson's reputation is that of honoring God, family values and patriotism. The only city in the world that compares to Branson in terms of being God focused is the Vatican (for different reasons). After traveling the country and ministering in 66 cities throughout the nation the Lord told us to speak into and pray into the established vision for Branson Missouri. Corrie Ten Boom saw an open vision of angels 5 levels deep over Branson. She declared God was going to do something special here. Nora Lam - the great Chinese evangelist saw angels standing protectively at the four corners of the Ozarks and prophesied a mighty move of God would come here. The same prophet who prophesied to Steve Hill about going to Pensacola and that he would see a mighty move of God - this same man (Michial Ratliff) prophesied over Branson that it would see a like outpouring. Others such as Maria Von Trapp, Billye Brim, Gwen Shaw, etc. have seen such things and come to Branson and the Ozarks in anticipation of what they were convinced God is going to do.

We are dependent upon the Holy Spirit: We cannot make this outpouring happen. But we can stand in testimony of it and speak into it, pray into it and lean into it with our faith. This prophesied revival will not happen if we merely wait and wonder and roll our eyes at every newcomer to our city seeking God's promise here. There are many in the area that hold themselves to be THE authority over the coming TRI-LAKES REVIVAL and they have fallen into skepticism and a critical spirit. We forgive them beforehand. This will not come with merely waiting and watching. We must DO something. Our faith is not measured by our words but our actions. This Tri-lakes Revival is not the Great Awakening but will serve as a staging ground, a launching place, a support to what is coming. It will be the "cloud the size of a man's hand" that Elijah saw when God told Him to get ready for a drought-ending downpour.

Jesus said in Luke 17:20,21 that the kingdom doesn't come with observation. We must do something. What must we do? John Wesley said "God will do nothing but in answer to prayer..." The Lord told me one day - *"I am perfect, sinless, resurrected, and at the right hand of the Father. If I have to pray - you have to pray"*. The works of God you are not praying into you do not believe in. Will you pray? Will you persevere in prayer? Will you pray "until"? We don't need a prediction or a prophecy to know we need a resurgence of godliness and spiritual hunger in our land and in the world. God is calling on us to pray out what He has already determined in His sovereignty to do. One writer in a book titled "Let us Pray" says this:

God communicates His will
We Discern His will as He has communicated it.
We return His will back to Him in Prayer.
Then He does His will in answer to prayer.

We all want change and see the need for change. Politics are not the answer. We are about to find that out - unequivocally in the next few years. The overthrow of the Federal government is not the answer (as some well-known ministers have suggested). I volunteered to work for Pat Robertson's presidential bid in the 80's and the Lord told me *"Go home you don't have permission to do this"*! I asked why and He gave me this verse:

Zec. 4:6 - It's not by might, not by power but by My Spirit says the Lord..."

It isn't that we can't get some things done in these arenas but the fact is - you cannot solve the problem on the level of the problem. You must ascend - and the path of ascension is in prayer. Do you see the threat to our faith in the earth today? We flew to the United Kingdom, and on the way over everyone was handed a piece of paper that said "*if you are coming to preach in the UK without government sanction we will turn you back at the terminal...*" Our legislative bodies, our presidents and military, our court systems are mocking our faith and thumbing their nose at gospel values. You can't solve the problem on the level of the problem and if you are waiting and watching ONLY you are a part of the darkness and not the light. We must DO something - and that is to pray.

There must be a prayer response. There are those called to focus your prayer efforts on the coming Great Awakening. There are those who are not involved at all in prayer groups that are to organize a prayer group that will ACTUALLY PRAY and not just say they pray. There are those that God wants to connect with the prayer initiatives available to you and become a part. Prayer changes things and THINGS ARE ABOUT TO CHANGE!

CHAPTER 7
AN OPENLY GAY PRESIDENT

Many of the things God spoke to me in this list of 24 events and happenings were not happy occasions. I give report of this to be faithful to what God showed me but honestly, I have no desire to alarm or disturb my brothers and sisters in Christ. I am so positive I'm dangerous. I am ready to charge hell with a water pistol. I believe in the unconquerable people of God. I have always told my wife Kitty that I want our ministry to be so positive that we make Joel Osteen look like Attila the Hun! The message of the gospel is the GOOD NEWS, not the pathetic picture of Chicken Little running around shouting "the sky is falling!"

There will be bleak seasons and hours of grim disappointment for the church and for the world. Fear not. We are on the winning team. The enemy is far more exhausted than we are. *The sky isn't falling the kingdom is coming.* God will work in the midst of chaos and upheaval to bring about His purposes. Now, why doesn't He explain Himself to us? Because He's bigger than we are, He knows more than we do and He's God! What seems like a setback, down turn or even outright defeat is actually God positioning His people to come to a place of humility and repentance so He can pour out a world changing, culture shifting, outpouring of His Spirit.

We are never truly at risk. What looks like down turn is simply an indication that we need to adjust our filter as the prophet Elisha, who saw the angels that his servant did not. When the servant's eyes were open he realized they were not outnumbered but in fact were in the majority!

Remember that God works in a 1000-years perspective. Many will read this book and think "isn't Jesus coming back before all this?" I don't think so. Now understand me clearly: He has my permission to come back before you read the end of this paragraph but - we are to occupy till He does come. If He tells us to occupy till He comes then we understand by inference that this is the perspective that God Himself takes. He builds and gets involved with the human race as though He isn't coming back for many millennia but He of course knows the day and the hour. In the meantime, we know that though things may look bad – God is setting us up for a great revival and major shift of the population of the world back to godliness. It has happened before and believe me it will happen again.

Yes, the Father did reveal to me that a homosexual president will sit in the Oval Office in my lifetime. This will not be a closeted gay person. This will be an openly gay President that will be sworn in without a bible, with his gay lover by his side. They will embrace in a passionate kiss in front of the Supreme Court Justice who swears him in and there will be a populist evangelical pastor standing by who is unable to resist the prestige of giving the blessing at a presidential inauguration. What a repugnant picture this is to the Evangelical community!

Just to digress a moment why do you think that the church has such a visceral reaction to the LGBT community? You might answer "well they are in sin!" Yes, to be sure they are – but God does not categorize sin or rank one sin as more obnoxious than another. Why doesn't the church have the same revulsion for gluttony, or gossip, or some of the many sexual proclivities that so often get exposed in our own ranks? What is it about homosexuality that pushes the button of an average Christian the way it does? Consider the following verse:

[Pro 27:19] 19 As in water face [answereth] to face, so the heart of man to man.

What is this saying to us? It is saying that when you look into the heart of man and see something other than what God sees, it is because you are identifying something in your own heart. When you look into someone's life and have a reaction that is other than the one that motivated the Father to send Jesus to the cross, it is because you are reacting to something in your own heart and life. This is the plain testimony of scripture even though it may not seem that the Evangelical community has ANYTHING in common with the LGBT society.

Let's consider this question. What is the core nature of homosexuality? Is it not a "like vs. like" attraction as the scripture says "man working with man that which is not convenient"? In other words, a homosexual claims they are only attracted to those that are just like them – a man to a man and a woman attracted to other women. They claim that is how God made them and how God wants it.

Is this not very much in common with how the church works? We only fraternize as believers with those who are just like us. They must believe like us and live like us and be just like us or we will not fellowship with them. In fact, for the most part the church believes that if you don't believe just like them you are going to hell! We have 16,000 denominations in Christianity that have spent billions of dollars to establish affinity societies, groups and churches in order to bring together people of "like" faith who believe like them, act like them and teach like them. We reject any who do not believe like us as "uninformed" at best and going to hell at worst. Furthermore – when you question religious leaders on this issue, they, like the LGBT community will say "this is how God made us, this is the way God wants it to be…"

Any honest Christian would see that the cookie-cutter demand upon the average believer is the bane of Christian culture as we know it. What is the difference therefore, in this regard between the LGBT community and the Christian community? In this instance, there is VERY LITTLE DIFFERENCE! Therefore, when the Evangelical church looks at homosexuals with revulsion rather than the love of Christ it is because they are judging their own selves and exposing the SPIRITUAL PERVSION in their own culture of DEMANDING and REQUIRING affinity as a basis of relationship and intimacy – just as a homosexual union requires.

Was it always this way? The early church was filled with people who came out of lifestyles of perversion and corruption. In the ancient world prostitution was a form of worship. Orphans in the ancient world survived by selling themselves as child-prostitutes to the upper classes sometimes from infancy. When these people came to Christ they had baggage that we would be hard pressed to over exaggerate. There were problems associated with this as well after they became believers. The Corinthian church blurred the line between *agape* love and the *eros* of sexual perversion. This was of course, corrected by the apostle Paul but it was done with a measured tone of love and fatherly influence and authority, not the shrill deprecations of a homophobic leadership. We need to lighten up not on sin but upon the self-righteous comparative attitudes we have toward homosexuals in the realization that much of the revulsion Christians feel toward the gay lifestyle is rooted in the hypocrisy of the church being the same way SPIRITUALLY as gay people are PHYSICALLY in their proclivities. Get the beam out of your own eye before you take the splinter out of your gay neighbor's.

Is it possible that a homosexual will sit in the White House? A decade ago this would have been utterly unfathomable. Today with the rapid inroads of the LGBT political lobby into the realm of politics and the church it isn't so far-fetched. Change is coming, and you will see these things in the not too distant future. Is this because the devil is gaining the upper hand? Far from it. Have you not read in the scriptures that where sin abounds grace does much more abound? Scandal will once again erupt in the halls of Evangelical institutions as the pedophilia scourge that has decimated the Catholic church will break out in the Southern Baptist convention. The Assemblies of God will swell in its numbers but become completely marginalized as a force for God. As an institution they will become an insipid parody of the great testimony they once held in their beginnings. Several high profile Assemblies of God ministers and churches will defect to non-denominationalism to distance themselves from an anemic headquarters leadership – all to no avail. The Assemblies of God is and will continue to grow into a defacto nominal denomination that has lost its power just as the Methodists of old experience in their time.

In rapid succession the social climate and the winds of political fortune will so orient this country that a gay president will become a foregone conclusion in an upcoming election. Those who disagree and voice dissent will be brutally turned back and silenced. The most conservative voices in this country will fall silent for fear of the political and social juggernaut that will bring this situation about. Political correctness will no longer be an obnoxious influence but the law of the land. Christians will be driven out of the public square by court edicts that make it impossible for them to maintain their faith and serve the public at the same time. State legislatures will be defeated time and time again as they vainly attempt to pass bills to protect the moral sense and decision making of Christian business people. Within 10 years Christian businesses will be completely unable to maintain their standards of morality without being bereft of their company's prosperity and bottom line. They will have to make a decision they will either capitulate to public policy or shutter their businesses. Wall Street will become dominated by LGBT influences and a near majority of Fortune 500 companies will have homosexuals at the helm.

How could all of this be brought about? As covered previously, in the years prior to this election there will be a very popular liberal woman in the oval office for two terms. This woman – and I don't know that it is Hilary Clinton but it might be - this woman will be hailed on both sides of the political isle as a great leader and economic powerhouse. On the heels of her success a homosexual front runner will emerge in a hotly contested presidential election. This rising homosexual political figure will not be a mere functionary or officer from the previous administration. This person will arise from the ranks of congress, specifically the House of Representatives. He will serve for some years as the minority whip and for one term as the majority leader of a Democratic controlled House. During this time the Senate will also be held by a liberal majority and the remaining term of this liberal woman will be anything but a lame duck. Legislation – far reaching legislations will be passed over the tepid and powerless objections of conservative politicians. There will be threats of overturning these laws and ousting incumbents, but it will be a vain threat for the country will have turned a page that will weaken the conservative party for decades to come.

The DNC will capitalize on the political cache of this very popular, liberal woman president and succeed in nominating and electing in a general election this homosexual man to the presidency of the United States. Coming from a conservative background with traditional family values this came as a shock to me. Surely God would never allow this to happen. You might ask why I would say such a thing – but know this: *I can only give you what God says to me and say it faithfully whether Christian culture and political pundits agree or not.* Change is coming. That hand of God is bringing justice to bear on the political scene because – and swiftly because the church has allowed itself to be prostituted by the political process. The RNC has deceived, manipulated and seduced the Christian and Evangelical electorate and their failure is imminent. I don't say this from any political bent or prejudice on my part. I have voted and supported conservative politicians and initiatives all my life but God is saying enough is enough. The pendulum is swinging radically to the left in this country far beyond any expectation we can conceive. Surely there will be reprieves, in fact two reprieves in the form of a Latino conservative who will come to the Whitehouse and a Conservative woman also who will serve two terms after this Latino leader. They will bring respite to the conservative movement as it struggles under the jack boot of the liberal agenda but there will not be lasting change for some decades. This is not just my word or my opinion but the word of the Lord as it comes from my mouth. Judge it as you will.

What I heard next was even more disconcerting: Not only is this going to be allowed to happen – it will be orchestrated by God's hand to exhaust the political appetites of the church and turn them back to prayer. For the church to put her hopes in the political process is foolhardy, and in fact it constitutes spiritual adultery. As the prophet said of old, when Judean kings looked to Egypt to save them "I will discover your skirts upon your face – and expose your false lovers ..." The RNC has manipulated and lied to the church – thinking it would use the Evangelical demographic as the DNC has successfully coopted the black vote in the United States. The difference is that the church bears the name of Christ and God takes it personally when the people of God give in and allow themselves to be seduced by the false dependencies represented by a vacillating, dishonest Conservative Movement and the RNC that has no honor and no more respect for the Evangelical movement than the DNC does for its own special interest groups.

When this gay candidate emerges on the world scene the Christian political machine will rise up in all its power and influence to stop this from happening. Old rivalries will be laid aside. The rift between the Catholic church in Europe and the Catholic church in North America will vanish as dioceses all over the world realize that the very foundation of their institution is being threatened by a liberal and socially amoral initiative that will be difficult to over exaggerate. Evangelicals will hold mass rallies and bitter denominational enemies will come into alliance around this homosexual threat. They will be totally confident that they can and will plow under the Presidential bid of this homosexual interloper. There will be many candidates in the conservative movement that will rush to the side of Christian conservatives and it will look like victory is at hand. Mark it down that the end result will be a total and transcontinental rout of Christian and Conservative values and institutions.

In spite of this Christians will take to the streets in record numbers. The capital mall will be flooded with sign waving, passionate Christian conservatives vowing never to allow such a travesty to happen. They will be utterly convinced that as a political force, the church of the Living God will be totally successful in thwarting the candidacy of this liberal homosexual for the Oval Office. They will be wrong. This man will win the presidency in a landslide victory that hasn't been seen since the days of Richard Nixon's second term. In the aftermath of this victory several denominations that identify as conservative and evangelical will renounce their values and standards against the LGBT lifestyle in a desperate bid to reacquire validity and relevance in a very different generation than Christianity has ever faced.

What possible good can come of this? Remember that God is God and ultimately He is in control. As the scripture plainly teaches us God sets up leaders and he removes leaders, and the powers that hold office do so in the context of His sovereign will. This belief will be SORELY tested for many years as the church and the RNC will suffer defeat after defeat. There will be strong talk and action taken to dismantle the RNC. Even in the courts law will be codified that will attempt to criminalize components of the RNC agenda and platform that are germane to LGBT interests. To be Evangelical and Conservative in years to come will be equivalent to being a member of the KKK.

These things will not happen for the purpose of destroying the church but to bring her back to her Anchor – the Lord Christ Jesus. God will woo the church back from her false lovers in the political arena and even in the military, for many Christians will call for the dismantling by force of arms the Federal government. This too will fail as God works in His mysterious ways to bring the church to repentance in preparation for a mighty outpouring of the Holy Ghost.

For decades the church has immersed itself in the seedy, back room machinations of the American political scene. Conservative, Beltway Republicans from the days of Ronald Reagan until now have signed on very openly to the values of the Christian conservative movement – only to betray, lie and obfuscate completely once they are in office. This is no different than what the DNC has done with the African American vote, the Women's lobby, etc.. The distinction is, however, regardless how politically misguided these people are – they are nonetheless God's people that are being manipulated by the RNC and conservative politicians at every level of government. God is a jealous God. He will trounce the RNC and bring them to an open shame. The continued existence of the Republican party will be held in genuine jeopardy for the first time in its history.

The Evangelical church and the Catholic church will come together like never before in this political foray, and will both be soundly defeated by their own constituency and will widely support this homosexual candidate. Why? Because this future gay leader of the free world is a very gifted legislator and because since the days of the Clinton scandal with Monica Lewinsky, personal values no longer matter in a material way when it comes to casting a vote for the leader of our nation.

CHAPTER 8

NATURAL DISASTERS

The Father says that a great natural disaster will strike the Midwest followed by the eruption of the Yellowstone caldera. Having been faithful to say this, let us recognize that it doesn't take any anointing to prognosticate natural disaster. Cataclysm, flood, earthquakes etc., happen all the time as Jesus spoke of in the gospel of Matthew:

> *[Mat 24:7 KJV] 7 For nation shall rise against nation, and kingdom against kingdom: and there shall be famines, and pestilences, and earthquakes, in divers places.*

In my vision I clearly saw the Yellowstone caldera going active and radically affecting the states bordering this part of the country. Air traffic will be rerouted for months dealing with the output of ash and volcanic material high in the sky and reaching around the globe. The effects of this volcanic activity will be measured in every quarter of the earth and will include a measurable drop in global temperatures. Temps will fall due to the atmosphere being darkened and the earth's weather systems will diminish as much as 1 degree on average worldwide. In the midst of this upheaval there will also be an economic boon to what happens in Yellowstone as geologists and fortune seekers will turn the calamity at hand into economic opportunity that will be identified and taken advantage of by those hardy enough to work in the conditions that will exist at that time.

When will this take place? Remember that prophets only see through a glass darkly. They hear in part and know in part. All I know is that these things have come to me as clearly as anything I have ever sensed in the prophetic throughout my life. God tells us to prophesy as His oracle yet directs that prophecy be judged and for those judging prophecy to remember it's obscure and imprecise nature. This is the plain teaching of Paul in 1 Corinthians:

> [1Co 13:12 KJV] 12 *For now we see through a glass, darkly; but then face to face: now I know in part; but then shall I know even as also I am known.*

Many might reject such a word and say it is fear mongering and pandering to the apocalyptic nature of weak minded people. To such a suggestion I can only point to the scripture. Did the prophets ever predict such events? Yes, they did. Did they ever warn people of such things to come? Yes, they did. We must be faithful to the heavenly vision. Elijah the Tishbite told king Ahab that there would be no rain except by his word because of unfolding events in the northern kingdom:

> [1Ki 17:1 KJV] 1 *And Elijah the Tishbite, [who was] of the inhabitants of Gilead, said unto Ahab, [As] the LORD God of Israel liveth, before whom I stand, there shall not be dew nor rain these years, but according to my word.*

Will these things happen because God is wrathful or mad at His people or the United States? I would suggest that God doesn't have to be angry for things such as earthquakes, volcanic eruptions and floods to take place. There is a such thing as causality in the earth. Things happen. Random events take place without any connection or meaning. I personally believe that all the wrath of God was poured out upon Jesus on the cross. The Father judged all sin in Christ on Calvary and did not spare any of His anger (in this dispensation) to heap upon the disobedient. Does that mean we don't have a choice? No – we can pray. If we pray many of these things will not take place. Of course if they don't happen, that makes me look like a false prophet – but rather to avoid calamity through intercession and prayer (as in Jonah's case) than to confirm catastrophe through prophetic pride and arrogance.

Before the eruption of the Yellowstone caldera there will be a wide spread natural disaster strike the Midwestern states. A flood of historical proportions will take place in the Mississippi River Valley that will defeat all efforts by the core of engineers to stem or control it. This flood will be a sign and a wonder preceding a Great Outpouring of God's Spirit in the United States that will radically effect an election that takes place a few years later.

In 2011 my wife and I had a front row seat to a locally devastating flood in Branson, Missouri. Our home was 50 feet from the water on the high side of the Taneycomo lake. As we watched homes being swept away and damage throughout the area the Father spoke the following to me that will find it's fulfillment in what is to come:

This is what I published at the time:

> *"My Kingdom is about to overflow its banks in the earth says the Lord. And those who have staked their future on existing boundaries are going to be displaced as I redefine the parameters of who I am and exactly what the mandate of My Kingdom is in the world of men. There will be men and women, good men and women who will experience the displacement and become spiritual refugees*

because they've been taken unawares. But the shift is necessary says the Father for I am enlarging My territory and expanding the floodplain of the River of My Glory into here-to-for untouched areas in the societies of men.

There have been those who have undertaken great projects to define and contain what I am doing and who I am in the earth says the Father. But I will not be tamed and I will not be contained. The river of My glory is breaking over all the barriers of men and flowing into the uttermost parts of the earth to inundate, shape and pour out upon even the most despised and rejected denizens of the earth.

I am calling this day for men and women who will receive a two-fold call: to address the refugee status of those who are about to be displaced from their comfortable vantage point on the river of My glory and to also allow themselves to be carried WHEREVER the current of My river flows to be My ambassadors and regents to those whose dry and thirsty lands are about to become lake front property on the banks of My redefined purposes in the earth.

For I have not called you to simply find your habitation in view of My glory says the Father. I am calling you to plunge into the billows and push out until your feet can no longer find the bottom. I will be your stay and I will be your sustaining breath as you allow yourself to be swept into the cataracts of My Kingdom deluge that I am bringing into the earth.

I am releasing My church from the boxes and boundaries that have contained them and spilling them out into the wild where they will reproduce and challenge the kings of the earth for the captives held in bondage by them. My servants, my handmaids and my prophets will surface in venues and marketplaces where they aren't invited but they will manifest My Glory and pour out the waters of My mercy and bring repentance, surrender and release to the captives of the earth till the entire spiritual geography of the earth shall be redrafted to take into account the work of My hands that I am doing even this day say the Father."

CHAPTER 9
THE UNION THREATENED

Years before the breakup of the Soviet Union, Pulitzer prize winner George Kennan predicted the Iron Curtain would fall. Kennan was a foremost architect of US foreign policy in modern times. His predictions came true. Ravi Batra, another award winning analyst and author not only predicted the Soviet Union would disintegrate he also predicted that capitalism as a form of government would likewise come to its end. He believed this would take place in the decade in which we are now living. It doesn't take a Harvard degree to perceive that there are social and economic pressures in the United States that are tearing at the fabric of our nation.

In 1983 CIA analyst Herb Meyer wrote an 8-page memo diagnosing symptoms of decline in the Soviet Union, and her eventual collapse. "The Soviet economy" Meyer contended, "is headed toward calamity" – we might add in retrospect irrevocably so. Part of the problem Meyer identified was a "demographic nightmare" that had to do with abortion rates at the time in the Soviet Union. The average Soviet woman at that time had at least six abortions. There are an average (since 1970) of 300+ abortions in the US for every 1000 live births. For Meyer, this statistic in the USSR pointed to a coming economic free fall in the years ahead. What about the

United States? 52 million babies have been aborted in the United States. What would our society look like – how different would things be just in our economy if there were 52 million more people within our borders with all the potential and economic possibility that they would represent?

Just looking at the state of affairs in our country in terms of the socio-economic ramifications of abortion, the outlook is not positive. As a people we can look back in history and decry the holocaust in Nazi Germany but make no mistake – the United States holds no moral high ground from the perspective of divine justice over the policies and government-led pogroms perpetuated by Hitler that killed fewer than have perished in the abortion clinics in our own nation since 1970. Perhaps we as a nation have become anesthetized to the horrors of abortion in our nation, but one could make the case that God overlooks such a travesty for any reason. The scripture tells us that God is indeed merciful but His Spirit will not always strive with man or with a nation that forgets God.

Augustine of old when writing on the breakup of the Roman Empire declared that God is not intrinsically invested in any nation or form of government. God is not a capitalist. God is not a Democrat or a Republican. He isn't even an American (as I found out after traveling and ministering extensively in Europe)! I met many sincere and deeply devout Europeans who loved God with all that was in them but at the same time they were staunchly anti-American in their sentiments. I had to make a decision if it was possible to be born-again and not be pro-American!

Augustine went on to contend in his classic tome "City of God" that the value of any form of government from a kingdom perspective is only established in the breadth by which it facilitates the preaching of the gospel of Jesus Christ around the world. I painfully remember crossing the Atlantic to visit our supporters in the UK only to see the warning on customs forms given to us before we landed: "If you are coming to do religious work without approval you will be turned back at Heathrow..." I was stunned. In the nation that sired Stanley and Livingston the gospel was being suppressed as a matter of foreign policy at even the very basic level of even entering the nation.

The United Kingdom is not unique in this regard. Years ago I remember my father – a devout minister and my "spiritual father" as well, coming to me after a season of prayer and meditation. "Persecution is coming to America" he told me. This was the late 80's. I couldn't imagine it. I prayed for many days asking the Father how could this be, and how would this begin. He reminded me of the Emancipation Proclamation that freed the black population in the south in the midst of the Civil War. For all the actions of the executive branch of government led by Lincoln, African Americans were brutally suppressed and persecuted for a 100 years afterwards. The Lord spoke clearly to me, that persecution in the United States would come through the judiciary branch of our government. Just a few days later I read in the paper of a house church pastor in Colorado Springs who was jailed for practicing his faith in violation of the covenants of the subdivision where his congregation gathered!

In the years that have passed since that time we have seen businesses destroyed, churches and ministries hauled before congress, IRS pogroms have raged against pastors and their congregations as people of faith have been herded into the ghetto of religion, and controls clamped down upon them to deny due process and freedoms that were once a forgone conclusion in our nation. In the 1970's homosexual churches were denied 501c3 status because they violated what the IRS termed to be "the public trust". The church applauded and approved. Now 30 years later churches and individuals of faith are being hounded and persecuted in the legislature and the judiciary, and our cries of "foul play" fall on deaf ears.

Dietrich Bonhoeffer, a theologian and pastor in the years of Nazi Germany wrote this:

> *"First they came for the Communists, but I was not a Communist so I did not speak out. Then they came for the Socialists and the Trade Unionists, but I was neither, so I did not speak out. Then they came for the Jews, but I was not a Jew so I did not speak out. And when they came for me, there was no one left to speak out for me."*

The Lord clearly spoke to me that in the next 50 years we would see the political and geographical integrity of our nation challenged to the breaking point. In November of 2012 the Huffington Post (never confused with a conservative voice in the annals of American journalism) reported that as of that date more than 30 states had met the threshold of due process for successfully filing to secede from the United States and the Federal government.

In Arlington, Texas just such a petition was filed with 60,000 signatures (only 25,000 are required for such a filing to be considered viable). The verbiage of the petition included the following language:

> *The US continues to suffer economic difficulties stemming from the federal government's neglect to reform domestic and foreign spending. The citizens of the US suffer from blatant abuses of their rights such as the NDAA, the TSA, etc. Given that the state of Texas maintains a balanced budget and is the 15th largest economy in the world, it is practically feasible for Texas to withdraw from the union, and to do so would protect its citizens' standard of living and re-secure their rights and liberties in accordance with the original ideas and beliefs of our founding fathers which are no longer being reflected by the federal government.*

What would a map of the region look like if the United States dissolved wholesale? Igor Panerin – a Russian professor and political scientist is best known for his hypothesis of what he terms "the possible breakup of the United States". Panarin further proposed a map of six geopolitical regions in the former United States that would be autonomous one from another and in socio-economic fidelity with Canada, China, Mexico, Russia and the European Union. Is this possible? Panerin accurately predicted the breakup of the Soviet Union and was hailed as visionary. Those same pundits have laughed him to scorn for suggesting that the US would suffer the same fate.

What does the bible say about the United States? It is ominously silent. Many prognosticators and scholars of biblical texts have made great efforts to identify the US among the nation states spoken of in the apocalyptic books of the bible. This is a very difficult thing because in fact the US is not mentioned and does not remotely figure largely if at all in the tableau of prophetic events described in Daniel, Revelation and elsewhere. There will be those that would argue this point – but not without postulating extreme, convoluted, and twisted reasonings that fall outside the bounds of accepted theological principles when it comes to eschatological inquiry. The writers of eschatological revelation in the Old and New Testaments describe the center of political, social and economic power in the earth at the time of the return of Christ to have predicted to be in south central Europe – a region completely unexplored and uncivilized at the time these things were written.

As Americans what is to be our response to such a suggestion? Be at peace in your heart. Regardless of what may or may not transpire in the United States – the sky isn't falling the kingdom is coming. Our security and safety is not dependent upon the contiguous solidarity of these United States. Ultimately our citizenship is in heaven and regardless what nations stand or fall – including the United States – God is in control!

CHAPTER 10
THE REPUBLICAN PARTY CHASTISED

The Father spoke to me that the leadership position of the Republican party in the United States is being removed. For 34 of the last 50 years the Republican party has dominated the executive branch of government and held the Oval office. During that time, prayer was taken from our schools. During that time, abortion was legalized, and since 1973 (under Republican largely administrations) 52 million abortions have been committed in the United States. Of course the GOP would point the finger at the Democrats and say this is all their fault because abortion is part of their platform, but it has been the Republicans who have held power for a majority of this time and as Harry Truman was fond of saying in the Oval Office – the "buck stops here".

The bishop prick (or staff) of the RNC is being taken from them. What does it mean to say that the "bishop's prick" of the RNC is being removed? This is a reference to Judas when the disciples decided to appoint another follower of Jesus to take Judas' place because he betrayed Jesus:

[Act 1:20 KJV] 20 For it is written in the book of Psalms, Let his habitation be desolate, and let no man dwell therein: and his bishoprick let another take.

The Republican party has betrayed the body of Christ in the US. Under Republican administrations our rights have been abrogated, and our freedoms curtailed. As Republican candidates eloquently champion Christian values with their words, our beliefs have been savaged, exploited and trampled upon. In all of this when the Christian electorate has cried out, the Republicans have clucked their tongues saying "that's too bad …" and suggesting that the answer is "4 more years!" God says, enough is enough. For 5 decades of obfuscation, political sleight of hand and outright betrayal, the Father will wrest the executive branch of government away from Republican candidates and give the Oval office largely to the DNC for the foreseeable future.

Does this mean that there will be no more Republican presidents? No, in fact there will be some bright stars that will come to power but they will not be beltway Republicans. The Republican establishment as of this writing is being dismantled by the ramifications and implications of the candidacy of Donald Trump for president. Whatever the outcome of the election, God has used Donald Trump to scourge the Republican party for its sins against the body of Christ. The Republican establishment has decried the P.T. Barnum character of the Trump campaign all the while working the same despicable tactics attempting to manipulate the Christian electorate (and other demographics) in a desperate bid to hold on to what God is removing from her grasp. Does that mean that the Republicans will lose the 2016 election? Probably so but I cannot say for certain because that isn't what God told me.

Will Hillary Clinton be the next president? I asked God that question directly, but He did not answer me. This is important to note. God does tell His prophets things to come. In the 2008 election every major prophetic voice in the US gave strong indications that they knew by the Spirit of God that Barack Obama would be the next president. Unfortunately, and tellingly, not one ministry or prophet came out and actually said this – for fear (no doubt) of losing their constituency. In the election that is in play right now, the prophets are strangely silent (at the time this was written). In the previous cycle it was astounding that the church would promote the leader of a patently false doctrinal system to be the leader of the free world.

In 2 Peter 2:19 we read that "of whom we are brought into bondage of the same we are overcome…" If Mitt Romney as a Mormon (a Christ rejecting religion) would have become President of the United States this country would have been overrun by cults, false doctrine and the spirit of Antichrist for decades to come. Barack Obama coming to power instead of Romney was the mercy of God extended to this nation. That is not to say I endorse Barack Obama or his policies but his presidency from a spiritual standpoint was a break fire against a spiritual tsunami of demonic force that would have been difficult to measure had Mitt Romney had been elected to the highest office of the land. It is astounding that Evangelical, Charismatic leaders and Christians endorsed and championed a Romney candidacy, being duped and misled by a corrupt and disingenuous Republican political machine to do so in 2008. Likewise, one cannot but question the convictions of Christian leaders endorsing a candidate who so evidently lacks (by any thoughtful metric) the godly character worthy of the churches' political support in the current 2016 election cycle. Apparently no compromise is too great in pursuit of forestalling the successful presidential bid of the opposing party.

Many would take issue with my assessment of the Mormon church or Romney himself. Let me assure you that my viewpoint is not arrived at lightly. I have had a very personal confrontation with the demons that lurk in the Mormon principality. The very text of the Mormon bible itself is inhabited and indwelt by a demon that would have been given power to destroy our faith and deceive this country wholesale, had Romney come to power. In spite of everything the Republican party and the Evangelical community did to the contrary, God in His mercy foiled Romney's candidacy and put President Obama in power.

Now we come to the election cycle again and the lessons of the past have not been learned. The RNC has taken its lessons from the liberal manipulation and coopting of the African American and other minority and special interests. The RNC looks upon the Christian community merely as a demographic to be manipulated in pursuit of political power. The candidates on the Republican platform praise God one day and curse Him the next – while the flags wave and the ongoing insistence continues that they are the party of God and country. Many will suggest that while the RNC is not perfect that they are a far better choice than the Democratic platform. It would be hard to disagree with that but here is the difference:

When the Democratic party manipulates and deceives its electorate that is one thing, and it is deplorable. When the RNC follows suit, and takes their cue from the Democratic playbook they seek likewise to deceive and manipulate the Christian electorate. Here is the difference – they have put God's name on the effort. They have branded themselves as the party of "God and Country". As previously stated over the years, I have heard many Christian Republicans remark that they just cannot see how someone could be born again and vote on a Democratic ticket. The hypocrisy of this opinion is difficult to over exaggerate. Ronald Reagan, whose record and history is increasingly being made public by the Reagan library was no friend of the Christian electorate. He stated plainly (and on more than one occasion) that while he promised otherwise he had no intention of giving the Christian demographic what he had publicly promised. The Christian community was something to be exploited and used to gain votes and nothing more.

[Num 11:1 KJV] ... and the LORD heard [it]; and his anger was kindled...

In the days of the kings of Israel when northern armies would invade and the kings of Judah would often call upon Egypt and other allies to come in and save them from being overrun. The Father would send prophets to warn the kings that sat on the throne of David not to put their trust in foreign powers:

> *[Jer 13:26-27 KJV] 26 Therefore will I discover thy skirts upon thy face, that thy shame may appear. 27 I have seen thine adulteries, and thy neighings, the lewdness of thy whoredom, [and] thine abominations on the hills in the fields. Woe unto thee, O Jerusalem! wilt thou not be made clean? when [shall it] once [be]?*

God is a jealous God. When His people put confidence in ANYTHING or ANYONE other than the Lord Jesus Christ, that constitutes spiritual adultery. The church has prostituted itself to the political process and it has in 50 years availed her nothing. The betrayal of the RNC against the church is measured in the disparity between the promises of her candidates and the deplorable assault on our faith that is increasingly more successful and continues unchecked despite the false promises of a deceptive and traitorous Republican National Committee.

What does this mean for us? We need to be reminded that our citizenship is in heaven. We need to be reminded that it is NOT BY MIGHT, NOR BY POWER but BY THE SPIRIT OF GOD that things get accomplished in the earth. We as a people, and as individuals must choose to put more confidence in what happens in our prayer closets than what is taking place in the voting booth. Does this mean we don't vote? Of course not. But when you vote – follow the leading of the Lord. Listen to His voice and do what He tells you. Refuse to be manipulated by the corrupt political machine, be it the RNC or the DNC. Your vote – like your life belongs to God. Do what you see the Father do and vote as you discern His directive to do so.

CHAPTER 11
ARABIC APOSTLES ARE COMING

The Father told me that out of the ranks of ISIS, and radical Jihadist movements, young Arabic apostles will be raised up. The apostle Paul in the first century was a persecutor of the faith and was very motivated to deliver Christians in the new movement over to torture and to death. He made Osama Ben Ladin look tame, compared to the rabid spirit of hate Paul demonstrated toward the early church.

> *[Act 9:1 KJV] 1 And Saul, yet breathing out threatenings and slaughter against the disciples of the Lord, went unto the high priest,*

In the western world we are very reticent to see anything good coming out of the Arabian Peninsula other than oil, and other miscellaneous commodities. Could God take a Jihadist – who has killed Christians, beheading them and displaying them in the most obnoxious and sickening way before the eyes of the world, and bring them to the cross? Remember this – God can do anything He wants anytime He wants and He doesn't have to check with anyone.

Was Paul God's first choice? Not likely. After the resurrection the apostles joined the 120 to wait for the promise of the Holy Spirit. They had no idea what Pentecost would mean or bring about. As they waited they began to sense a lack of order in their ranks, and inquired among themselves as to what might be amiss. No doubt, they thought as they waited that perhaps some disobedience on their part was causing an unnecessary divine delay. Finally, their attention fell to the matter of Judas. They now numbered 11 and not 12. Perhaps (they conjectured) there was a need to restore and appoint a 12th disciple. Could this be the key to provoking what Jesus called "the promise of the Father" that they were all waiting upon?

We have no indication whether or not this was God's will (that Judas be replaced by apostolic election of the remaining disciples). Apparently this was just a good idea brought on out of fear that they were going to miss God's visitation unless something was done to restore what they considered good order. In order to proceed what did they do? Acts 1:15-26 give us the details:

[Act 1:15-26 KJV] 15 And in those days Peter stood up in the midst of the disciples, and said, (the number of names together were about an hundred and twenty,) 16 Men [and] brethren, this scripture must needs have been fulfilled, which the Holy Ghost by the mouth of David spake before concerning Judas, which was guide to them that took Jesus. 17 For he was numbered with us, and had obtained part of this ministry. 18 Now this man purchased a field with the reward of iniquity; and falling headlong, he burst asunder in the midst, and all his bowels gushed out. 19 And it was known unto all the dwellers at Jerusalem; insomuch as that field is called in their proper tongue, Aceldama, that is to say, The field of blood. 20 For it is written in the book of Psalms, Let his habitation be desolate, and let no man dwell therein: and his bishoprick let another take. 21 Wherefore of these men which have companied with us all the time that the Lord Jesus went in and out among us, 22 Beginning

from the baptism of John, unto that same day that he was taken up from us, must one be ordained to be a witness with us of his resurrection. 23 And they appointed two, Joseph called Barsabas, who was surnamed Justus, and Matthias. 24 And they prayed, and said, Thou, Lord, which knowest the hearts of all [men], shew whether of these two thou hast chosen, 25 That he may take part of this ministry and apostleship, from which Judas by transgression fell, that he might go to his own place. 26 And they gave forth their lots; and the lot fell upon Matthias; and he was numbered with the eleven apostles.

Notice that it was Peter, who pondered the scriptures and decided that another disciple should be appointed. Peter didn't didn't necessarily have a track record of coming up with good suggestions (get thee behind Me Satan – was Jesus' response to the last one he made before this). No doubt he was attempting to appear as a strong leader, having been singled out by Jesus as the chief among the newly called apostles. Peter quotes a few verses, and then lots were drawn among the eligible followers of Jesus for one to replace Judas. In other words, they drew straws! I wonder if Matthias got the long straw or the short straw! In any case Matthias was chosen to sit in the seat of witness that had originally belonged to Judas. Remember now, that Judas was chosen by the Lord Himself and now Matthias is chosen by the 11 in Jesus' absence while they waited in the upper room for whatever Jesus had promised – hoping that this choice would hasten things along.

Whatever happened to Matthias? His appointment was unique, because he wasn't appointed by Jesus and that his selection took place before the descending of the Holy Spirit upon the church. After this singular mention, Matthias is not reference again in the canonical gospels or the epistles that came after. There are many legends about what became of him, but from the sacred narrative itself we can presuppose that his apostleship was unremarkable at best – a total mistake at worst.

Then there is the matter of the stoning of Stephen, and a young man by the name of Saul who stood by sanctioning this brutal mob execution. Whatever Saul witnessed of Stephen's face shining like an angel, it did not stop him from requesting permission to carry out persecution in the north country. He actually hails from Damascus and it is to Damascus that he now travels intending slaughter and persecution against any Christians that he might find there.

Imagine this happening today? A Syrian Jihadist travelling the countryside, killing and imprisoning believers with the sanction of Middle Eastern religious authorities who are not friendly to the Christian faith. Sound familiar? Well know this brothers and sisters that there will come apostles out of the ranks of Jihad to preach the gospel with the spirit and power of an apostle Paul. The blood of the martyrs that has been spilled in Syria and Iraq by ISIS radicals will so haunt their killers that they will only find respite and deliverance in a Damascus road experience no less astounding or remarkable than that which Paul experienced himself 2000 years ago.

God will raise up 8 apostolic reformers inspired to come to Christ by the martyrdoms of young westerners. At the time God first gave this to me there were no young western martyrs known to have died in ISIS captivity. Just a few months afterward Kayla Mueller, a 26-year-old humanitarian worker from Prescott, Arizona died at the hands of her ISIS captors. There were rumors that she read the bible, and sang Jesus Culture songs to those that brutalized her. Within just a few months ISIS terrorists began to trickle in to aid stations in Syria and Iraq to turn themselves in and come to Jesus because they were under such heavy conviction of the Holy Ghost.

We haven't seen anything yet. 2 of the 8 apostles God is raising up from Syria and Iraq will be young women who will lay down their Kalashnikov rifles and take up the emblem of the cross with great power, and signs and wonders. All of these young people will be younger than 35 years of age. We will see the first instance of this in just a few short months. These ministers will make their way to the United States in spite of being on no-fly lists. Homeland Security will try to apprehend them and be unable to lay hold on them though they will stand in their midst. Those they do imprison will be delivered by angels, as Peter of old and the uproar will set the secular powers of our society into an apoplectic fit.

These roaring young reformers will leave the so-called apostolic leaders of the western church in total disarray, and unable to reply to the burning intensity of these passionate young disciples. They will speak not only from the scriptures but give testament to a living Christ who will attend their preaching with signs, wonders and miracles. They will be called false, Jihadist spies, anti-Christ, etc., but their ministries will be vindicated supernaturally in ways unprecedented in modern times.

How are we to respond to such events? By knowing that the sky isn't falling, the kingdom is coming. God is not a westerner. God is not an Anglo-American. Neither is he a capitalist or a socialist. The kingdoms of this world are set to become the kingdoms of our God and his Christ. These young apostles will be the first wave of an apostolic reformation that contrasts itself from the institutional church in much the same intensity as the early church was distinguished from the Judaism that crucified Jesus. Keep your heart open. Trust God to lead and to confirm. Cry out to Him to keep you relevant and connected to what He is doing no matter what the cost or how many stereo-types or sacred cows of doctrine or culture you are required to lay down.

CHAPTER 12
ETHNIC JUSTICE PREVAILS IN THE EARTH

For most people born to the white majority, race is not an issue in their everyday life. We hear terms like "white privilege" and simply can't relate to it other than as a politically driven issue that doesn't represent our everyday values. Does God care about race or ethnicity? We all remember the Sunday School rhyme "red and yellow, black and white – they are precious in his sight..." but does the issue of ethnicity emerge as anything other than this simplistic sentiment? In the last year events in Ferguson and many other communities coast to coast are a wakeup call to all Americans about a coming racial shift in the United States. We are within one or at the most two generations of seeing the white majority become for the first time in our history a minority in our country. The implications of this are staggering and the pace of this shift is exponentially accelerating.

With shift comes upheaval and nobody likes change or takes it very well. Those that are entrenched in the status quo see any tectonic transition in society as not serving their interests. Why would white America embrace change when the status quo has served us so well? If Hispanic and African-American interests suddenly reflect the majority opinion in this country what does this mean for the majority? The seeds of this change were planted 500 years ago when a Hispanic by the name of Columbus became a key player in bringing the African slave trade to the western world and to North America in particular. The pendulum swings and as God takes His 500 year strides He is looking out upon the racial tableau of the Western World and His hand is moving to bring justice and adjudication to the impoverished and disenfranchised peoples of the west, particularly in the United States. Why would it happen here first? Because we call ourselves "one nation under God" and words mean something. Judgment first comes to the house of God.

Does this mean that God is mad at white people? Far from it. Are white people the only oppressors among the peoples of the earth? Hardly. But God in His wisdom has crafted the anchor points of His kingdom to sink down and be established in the earth not only to the advantage of the white majority but the other racial groups as well. Of course when we talk race and religion many ancient and obnoxious issues are stirred up. Most theologians and church leaders would NEVER address these issues because they are inherently caustic and difficult. However, to ignore this issue is, at a very basic level to completely marginalize an important aspect of the gospel that is INTRINSICALLY racial in its implication, scope and import. The church is not to be silent on this issue. It is not acceptable for the racial divides in our culture to be blindly accepted by those who claim to walk in the light. God is moving by His hand to strike a parity of racial justice in the earth and the church will not escape the implications of His purposes as they come about. Jesus declared that before the end comes and the kingdom is consummated, that the gospel must first be preached. He not only declared that the gospel must first be preached but He specified that it must be preached to a very specific set of demographics and in a very particular scope of issues:

[Mar 13:10 KJV] 10 And the gospel must first be published among all nations.

The word "nations" here is not speaking of territories or boundaries. The word there is "Ethnos" or "Ethnicities". Like it or not, the gospel has an ETHNIC COMPONENT that has been totally marginalized and ignored by church leaders and theologians. It isn't convenient. Race issues are a minefield no one wants to step into. Yet Jesus says "like it or not - till you preach THIS COMPONENT of the gospel I'm not coming back..." We can preach to individuals, we can bring the gospel to age groups and special interest groups, we can even rehash the gospel endlessly to those who have already heard it, but until the gospel is preached as it applies to the ethnicities of the earth it has not been fully declared.

How does the kingdom come to bear on the ethnic groups of the earth? Well, it is important to remember that in centuries past national boundaries were more defined by their peoples than their territories. Having made that distinction, it then sheds new light on how God dealt with nations as we search specific instances out in the biblical narrative. When God was dealing with nations He was dealing with ethnicities and people groups, not territories and land masses. This distinction cannot be overemphasized or understated. When God instructed Moses regarding the Amorite people, he was warned not to engage with them because it was not their time yet. In other words, there is a time and a season apportioned and appointed to every people group of the earth.

[Gen 15:16 KJV] 16 But in the fourth generation they shall come hither again: for the iniquity of the Amorites [is] not yet full.

There will come a time in the earth for each ethnic group or people group that their time will be full. This is true of Judaism and of all non-Jews classed as "Gentiles" and it is true of each subgroup under the non-Gentile heading. The precedent for this is the reference to the fullness of time where the Amorites are concerned and many other references as well. Jesus spoke eloquently of this in the gospel of Luke:

> [Luk 21:24 KJV] 24 And they shall fall by the edge of the sword, and shall be led away captive into all nations: and Jerusalem shall be trodden down of the Gentiles, until the times of the Gentiles be fulfilled.

There is a time and a season appointed for the black race. There is a time and a season appointed to the Hispanic peoples. There is a time and a season for the Asian races, the White race and other people groups as well such as First Nations people in Canada and Native American peoples in the US. God will not leave you where you are at. Shift will come. Those in the minority will come to promotion. Those in the majority will be called upon to humble themselves to a minority position, and to make themselves a blessing and not a curse to majority races coming to the forefront. As believers we must choose to be a part of the solution and not part of the problem, as God adjudicates for the peoples of the earth in ALL our best interests and not just a few regardless of color, creed or ethnicity.

These changes and shifts will begin to emerge very prominently in the next half century. According to the Pew foundation - Latinos now surpass whites as the largest ethnic/racial group in California and New Mexico. What does that mean? White folks are now a MINORITY GROUP in California and New Mexico. According to Pew's statisticians Texas will soon follow. Whites have been in the minority in Hawaii for some time (22.8% white compared to 46.1% Asian or Pacific Islander). Does this matter? Ask the people in Ferguson, Missouri where recent events boiled over into riots fueled by frustration over the race disparity between African-Americans and the predominantly white law enforcement agencies that police that city.

What is white privilege? A good question to think about considering the fact that demographers predict that non-Hispanic white people as racial group will become a minority by 2043. God has revealed that it will be much sooner than this. What does this have to do with the gospel? Is it inappropriate to bring this up in a religious venue? In Mark 13:10 Jesus defines the gospel as good news to the NATIONS (gr. ETHNOS). God is a God of justice. Throughout the scripture God consistently moves to strike social parity among nations. We have been seeing this trend for some time beginning with the Native Americans, and now Hispanics and African Americans.

President Obama was elected not only by the electorate. The scripture declares that God raises up leaders in His sovereignty. The first minority to sit in the Oval Office was a black man. The western world as we know it during and before the industrial revolution was built upon the backs of slave labor. African slaves came to North America beginning with Columbus 500 years ago. God steps through time (it has been said) in 500 year increments. In North America even before the travesty of the decimation of Native American peoples, African slaves were employed to the benefit of their masters in this land through the brutality of the institution of slavery. First in suffering - first in promotion.

For those of us in the Non-Hispanic white demographic this should give us cause to reflect. We want to be part of the solution and not part of the problem (or not?). The xenophobic attitudes regarding race and immigration issues have been draped in the flag of patriotism for too long. That won't wash if we are a KINGDOM PEOPLE FIRST - Americans second. God is not a Republican. Neither is He a Democrat. He isn't a white God or a black God either. This isn't a political issue it is a kingdom issue and it is time to for believers of every race to break the protocols of social expectation, prejudice, political correctness and cultural bias and open a dialogue with those of opposing ethnicities in hopes that we as a diverse people can cooperate and acknowledge what God is doing lest we find ourselves resisting the work of His hands.

CHAPTER 13
SHIFTING WHITE MAJORITY

In 1588 the Spanish armada sailed against England and was defeated in what became known as the Battle of Gravelines. Of the 130 ships sent by Philip II to overthrow Elizabeth many failed to return being sunk by English fire ships, and even the weather itself conspired against them, sinking many in their retreat. The naval might of Spain was defeated and Hispanic history pushed back to the margins of importance as English strength surged forward to take the stage and establish an empire upon which the sun never set. Had Philip been successful and another outcome secured – Spanish may well have become the language of the modern world instead of English.

As pointed out in earlier chapters, God seems to step through time and history in 500 year increments or strides. In our day we now see the Hispanic peoples of the earth on the rise and flourishing in every major economy in the western world. In the US itself as of 2014 the majority of children now born within our borders are of a minority extraction. At current birth rates and taking into consideration immigration statistics, many demographers predict that in the next many decades Hispanic people will outnumber the white majority throughout our country. Whether this actually plays out or not, it is obvious to even the most casual observer that the Hispanic community in the United States is coming to promotion.

The Father spoke clearly to me that He is bringing His purposes in the Hispanic community to a tipping point. What we are seeing in the US and the Western world is not just the consequence of a failed immigration policy. The ethnic balance of history is shifting. What it means to be in the white majority in this country is changing. One of the primary beneficiaries of this shift is and will continue to be the Hispanic peoples in all their diverse people groups. Upon hearing this declaration echoed in the words of the Father I began to ask why this is coming about? As my wife Kitty often says *"anything that makes you do a double-take, pray to interpret..."* You don't have to be a prophet or claim to hear from God to see something happening in the Hispanic community. 2 of the 4 presidential candidates in the current election year (2016) are Hispanic. In the 113th congress there are 33 Hispanics serving in the legislature, shaping the policies and future of our nation. In just a few short decades, the Hispanic demographic is now the largest minority group in the United States surpassing even the African American people who have historically held that distinction.

Think about this in terms of spiritual principles. Hispanic people come to this country and they take the jobs that no one will take. They work for pay that no other ethnicity would accept or even consider. By coming in low and doing what no other people group as a whole would be willing to do, the Hispanic people have inadvertently activated the principle found in Matthew 20:16:

[Matthew 20:16 KJV] 16 So the last shall be first, and the first last: for many be called, but few chosen.

In 2012 Kitty and I had the privilege of ministering in a large Hispanic church in an impoverished area of Houston. After preaching, the people came forward to personally give of their meager offerings. As they passed by laying their offerings on our open bibles the pastor explained *"they want to give to you personally ... they want to honor you..."* The people filed by with tears in their eyes asking us to touch their children, to pray over those bound in wheelchairs, even to autograph their bibles. It was deeply humbling and very revealing of their character. Over the years we have seen this repeated time and time again.

> *The Father says that the innate humility in the Hispanic people has moved My hand to respond and bring them to greatness in the earth and specifically in the United States.*
>
> *1 Pe 5:6 KJV - Humble yourselves therefore under the mighty hand of God, that he may exalt you in due time:*

God has an automatic response to humility. The Hispanic peoples in the western world have occupied the low place. They have been greatly despised and exploited in the United States but the Father says:

> *Isa 57:15 KJV - For thus saith the high and lofty One that inhabiteth eternity, whose name [is] Holy; I dwell in the high and holy [place], with him also [that is] of a contrite and humble spirit, to revive the spirit of the humble, and to revive the heart of the contrite ones.*

The Pew Research Foundation states that in recent years the Hispanic community has exploded in growth to being the second largest people group in the US. Census data (after the white majority) and Pew's research indicates that at the current rate of growth the Hispanic community will become THE MAJORITY ethnicity in the United States in just a few years.

I asked the Father what this meant.

He said that within three election cycles the Hispanic community will have the opportunity not only to determine who sits in the White House but to place a Hispanic leader in the Oval Office.

This man will be a conservative, but his loyalties will be to his God before any political ideology or creed.

The mantle of majority in this country is passing to the Hispanic community in the United States and your eyes will see it and you will reap the rewards, as you align yourselves with God's purposes in this next season. When praying about this the Father spoke this to my heart:

The Hispanic community in the United States is coming to promotion.

The Father is bringing His purposes in the Hispanic community to a tipping point in the year 2013 and the years beyond. I asked Him why this was going to happen:

The Father said there is an innate humility in the Hispanic people that has moved My hand to respond and bring them to greatness in the earth and specifically in the United States. Those in whom humility is found will find themselves thrust into the DUE TIME of God's mighty hand.

Jam 4:6 KJV - But he giveth more grace. Wherefore he saith, God resisteth the proud, but giveth grace unto the humble. God resists (sets his forces in array against the proud) but gives grace (His empowering presence) to the humble.

The invitation of the King of Kings to the Hispanic community is reflected in:

Luk 14:10 KJV - But when thou art bidden, go and sit down in the lowest room; that when he that bade thee cometh, he may say unto thee, Friend, go up higher:

Why is this going to happen? Because you (if you are of Hispanic extraction and reading this) have occupied the low place. You have been despised and used and looked upon as a commodity to be exploited.

The Father says over the Hispanic peoples of the earth "Enough is Enough!"

In Zech. 2:8 the Father says that you are as the apple (or pupil) of His eye. When someone touches you or puts his finger in your eye you have an automatic response to defend yourself. Likewise, when the Father finds humility in your heart, He will move to DEFEND, PROTECT, PRESERVE AND PROMOTE YOU. The word HUMILITY in the bible means to GO LOW.

Have you ever watched the weather on TV and noticed that the rain clouds always gather to the LOW place in the atmosphere? Jesus said the kingdom works just this way:

Mat 16:3 KJV - And in the morning, [It will be] foul weather to day: for the sky is red and lowring. O [ye] hypocrites, ye can discern the face of the sky; but can ye not [discern] the signs of the times?

Jesus is saying to us that by learning about how our weather system works we learn how the kingdom works. There are seven great jet streams of wind that circle the earth, creating our weather. Meteorologists will tell you that when those winds encounter a low pressure zone they will pour out of their beneficial rains in that area. Likewise, just as there are seven natural winds that bring the beneficial rains to the LOW places of the earth – even so Isa. 11:1-3 says that there are SEVEN SPIRITS OF GOD that respond to those who are GOING LOW and walking in humility.

When the Father finds humility in your life or in a people the seven spirits of God bend low and pour out the rains of the Holy Spirit upon that people to bring them to their destiny. What are the seven Spirits of God? Isa. 11:1-3 tells us they are the Spirit of the Lord, the Spirit of Wisdom, Understanding, Counsel, Might,

Knowledge and the Fear of the Lord. God begins with the Spirit of the Fear of the Lord and causes us to ascend in worship to the knowledge, might, counsel, understanding, wisdom and finally the Spirit of the Lord Himself, activated over you as a people to bring you to your destiny. These are even as the rungs of the ladder that Jacob saw at Bethel in the night when he was fleeing from Esau.

Luk 19:26 KJV - For I say unto you, That unto every one which hath shall be given; and from him that hath not, even that he hath shall be taken away from him.

God is taking the bishop's staff of majority in this country and leadership rule from that people who have largely in recent years proved themselves unworthy of it and passing it on to the Hispanic community because the Father has found an humility in the Hispanic people He can work with to bring His glory.

Observations and Conclusions: Again - the Pew Research Foundation states that in recent years the Hispanic community has expanded in growth to being the second largest people group in the US. Census data and Pew's research indicate that at the current rate of growth the Hispanic community will become THE MAJORITY ethnicity in the United States in slightly less than one generation. The Hispanic community will have the opportunity not only to determine who sits in the White House but to place a Hispanic leader in the Oval Office. This man will be a conservative but his loyalties will be to his God before any political ideology or creed. The bishop's staff of growth, blessing and leadership is passing from its existing hands to the Hispanic community in the United States and your eyes will see it.

CHAPTER 14
AN AFRICAN-AMERICAN ELITE

God works in a time frame of history. We have just passed the 500th year that persons of African descent have been exploited on the North American continent. When Columbus navigated to the western hemisphere the Nina was piloted by an African sailor and a slave served as Columbus' cabin boy. Long before the first Native American laid eyes on a white man African slaves were the stock and trade of the European nations whose enforced labor was an indispensable component of the development of the western world. By 1867 more than 12.7 million men, women and children of African descent had been sold on the auction blocks of North America and the United States. From that perspective the social debt incurred by the western world upon African peoples is starkly apparent.

God is a God of unilateral fairness who adjudicates in His purposes for ALL the peoples of the earth – not just a privileged majority. This includes ethnicity, class, gender and nations. One of the core values of the kingdom of God and our heavenly Father is His inalienable sense of justice. The Father is committed to a campaign of ethnic justice in the earth. The injustices that religion, government and manifest history has failed to correct God is now moving to address. As God heard the cry of His people under

Pharaoh and sent deliverance, He likewise has heard the cry of the African-American people and is answering in His sovereignty.

In Matt. 28:19 and Mark 13:10 Jesus stated that the gospel is the Gospel to the nations. That word NATIONS is the word ETHNOS from which we also derive the word ETHNICITY. It is a fundamental truth that the gospel is a gospel of salvation from injustice, from bondage, from exploitation, and where that has existed God will right the balances working from an economy of scale spanning not just decades but centuries.

In ancient Israel there was a famine that would not lift in King David's time. When consulting the prophets and the Urim and Thummim it was discovered that an ethnic injustice from long before required correction in order to bring God's blessing on the land again:

> *[2Sa 21:1-3 KJV] 1 Then there was a famine in the days of David three years, year after year; and David enquired of the LORD. And the LORD answered, [It is] for Saul, and for [his] bloody house, because he slew the Gibeonites. 2 And the king called the Gibeonites, and said unto them; (now the Gibeonites [were] not of the children of Israel, but of the remnant of the Amorites; and the children of Israel had sworn unto them: and Saul sought to slay them in his zeal to the children of Israel and Judah.) 3 Wherefore David said unto the Gibeonites, What shall I do for you? and wherewith shall I make the atonement, that ye may bless the inheritance of the LORD?*

It has been said that God moves in 500 year strides through history. This can be described as God's linear purpose through time. There were approximately 500 years between the writing of the book of Malachi and the coming of Jesus. There were 500 years from the crucifixion of Jesus to the fall of the Roman empire. 500 years later the schism between the Eastern Orthodox Church and the Western Roman church was formalized, laying the foundation for the cultural divide between east and west in the modern world. 500 years after that Martin Luther came on the scene at the same time Columbus opened the New World to Christianity. 500 years later a man of African descent becomes the leader of the free world and of the most powerful nation on the earth.

Beyond the scope of President Obama's ideology, beyond the political machinations of the right or the left, conservative or liberal, President Obama's election signals the fullness of time in God's campaign of ethnic justice in behalf of all peoples of African descent in the western world and African-American people in particular. To those who resent President Obama's election I refer you to the following scripture:

[Dan 2:20-21 KJV] 20 Daniel answered and said, Blessed be the name of God for ever and ever: for wisdom and might are his: 21 And he changeth the times and the seasons: he removeth kings, and setteth up kings: he giveth wisdom unto the wise, and knowledge to them that know understanding:

Proverbs 16:33 tells us that man may cast a lot but God decides the outcome. Man may pull the voting lever but God holds the key to the executive washroom in the Oval Office. The apostle Paul commanded us:

[1Ti 2:1-3 KJV] 1 I exhort therefore, that, first of all, supplications, prayers, intercessions, [and] giving of thanks, be made for all men; 2 For kings, and [for] all that are in authority; that we may lead a quiet and peaceable life in all godliness and honesty. 3 For this [is] good and acceptable in the sight of God our Saviour;

To those who have rejected President Obama and fantasized about the military overthrow of the government or the assassination of our current president, I submit to you that your problem is not a political problem or a Democratic problem but a God problem. For 50 years the conservative party has dominated the Executive Branch of Government and they have largely done so by coopting the theme of God and country. The Republican party has seduced the church to exchange the altar of prayer for the political action committee. The church of the living God has thus been reduced to the profane status of a marginalized Washington special interest group. The Republican party has manipulated the Christian electorate by blaming the Democrats for all the social ills in our society while they themselves have not delivered on ONE ITEM of the Christian political agenda, from the inception of the Moral Majority under Jerry Falwell right down to today. Instead, they vilify the Democratic party and claim the only answer is "Four more years…" Because of this, and because they have denigrated the people of God and the name of Christ to a mere political tool – the Father says that the BISHOP PRICK, THE BISHOP'S STAFF of the executive branch of government has been taken from the conservative right and given to the political left for the next fifty years.

You may look at the second term of President Obama's tenure and think that this time is coming to an end. This is not the ending of something but the beginning of something. The tenure of President Obama has been like a birth canal to birth God's purpose in the African-American people. Just as Herod came against the children of promise, so as with the Travon Martin case, African-American young people have not been as vulnerable as they are today since the 60's and 70's. Once again black Americans no longer feel safe on the streets of our cities. Racial profiling, rampant crime rates and the disintegration of the African American family unit all contribute to the relative insecurity and frustration of Black America. We can look to the political arena or the courts to remediate this problem but in the final analysis this is God's problem and He has a ways and means committee to adjudicate on behalf of the African American people. God's purpose will not be denied.

The word of God over the African American people is:

First in Suffering – First in Promotion:

From this time forward you are going to see African-American men and women moving to the forefront of every major field of endeavor in western culture. Not just in sports, but in Finance, Business, Government, the Military, Entertainment, Medicine, Education, the Arts and Religion as well. Since this word was first given we have seen Lester Holt surprisingly take the place of Brian Williams at the helm of the most respected network news program in the US. African-American men and women will not just be the beneficiaries of the bounty of these realms but they will increasingly be the decision makers, influencers and movers and shaker across every strata of western society as God rights the scales of ethnic justice in their behalf.

First in Suffering – First in Promotion:

It is not by mere chance that an African-American man is the first minority to sit in the oval office. Before a woman or a Hispanic or other minority, God used an African-American to go before and breakthrough in behalf of other people groups. In the next ten election cycles you will see a Hispanic man and an Anglo woman in the White-house but the forerunner in this and every other major field of endeavor for the next half-century will be African-American men and women, chosen not by man or by the church but by the Father because He is God and He can do anything He wants any time He wants and He doesn't have to check with anybody.

Two Anglo Prophets – God's chosen messengers:

God didn't chose to deliver this message through a minority ministry but through two Anglo-Americans. You see when David summoned the Gibeonites, he knew the famine wouldn't lift until the

Gibeonites blessed their former oppressors in the name of the Lord. Therefore, God sent two white people with this message in order that the cultural divide between black and white would be closed by an act of humility through two unsung, unknown prophetic servants.

The Father told us in 2009 that we would prophesy to "people groups and people groups and people groups". This includes African-Americans, Hispanics, and Anglos. In 2012 Dr. Rosalys Martinez invited us to speak to a conference of Hispanic churches and to bring "the prophetic word to the Hispanic People". This was the beginning of the fulfillment of the prophecy in 2009 whereby we have prophesied to audiences of up to 30 million Hispanic believers. This conference was held in the church home of an African-American congregation. The pastor came up afterwards and asked "when are you going to prophesy to OUR PEOPLE". Just as Dr. Rosalys asked for the Hispanic people and that word was delivered so when this pastor asked there came an answer. When you ask the prophet it will be God that answers. When you can't ask your prophet because you don't want him or her to speak about something, you inform them about then you don't want a prophet you want a psychic. But God sent two Anglo prophets to bring the gospel of Ethnic Justice to the Hispanics likewise He sent us to the African-American people with this GOOD NEWS.

The Gibeonites were a slave people. God cares for the disenfranchised of the earth. Whether man cooperates or not – God is sovereign. The cries you have cried out with for your children and your children's children not will be ignored but are being answered. You might ask what about the return of Christ? Jesus said "occupy till I come…." Expect him to come tomorrow but work and plan like He isn't coming for a 1000 years. I have news for you: that is how God himself conducts His business. Go ahead and dream. Go ahead and plan says the Father for I am with you both to will and to do My good pleasure.

CHAPTER 15
FROM WHITE PRIVILEGE TO SERVANT SONS

In 2009 my wife Kitty and I were working in the IT business in the small Midwestern town of Clinton, Missouri. For years in business I didn't mingle spiritual pursuits with business concerns, but this year God introduced me to the idea of "market place ministry". We understood that it was not wise to mix "business and religion" but one could however, walk in the kingdom in the arena of business and see a new dynamic of faith made manifest. That being our conviction we added on to our small business an internet café for the singular purpose of creating a social setting where we could interact with our customers and gain an opportunity to share Jesus with them in the midst of the ebb and flow of the business transactions that were otherwise taking place.

The result was dramatic and almost immediate. Long standing customers that I had never shared my faith with were asking for prayer at the check-out counter. We would carry equipment out to our customer's cars and they would stand with their keys in their hands weeping as we prayed for them and the needs in their lives. Several customers wanted to know where we attended church, and would we start a bible study to minister to their needs? At first we were reluctant. We didn't want this fresh and new thing that God was doing to morph into a "churchy" type ministry. Eventually however we did start to hold meetings and this constituted the beginning of what would become Father's Heart Ministry. In the midst of this we remained committed to our business and saw that as the center of what the Father had called us to. This would soon change.

On a particular day in late summer the Father spoke to me to drive 100+ miles south to a home meeting that was taking place in Springfield, Missouri. I had received an e-mail invitation, but because it was a week day and we had to work the next day I didn't consider attending. There was to be a prophet and apostle team from Texas whose names I didn't recognize, that were to be the guest speakers. At the suggestion that we make the effort to drive this distance and attend I waited on the Lord a few moments and felt the confirmation in my spirit that yes, this is what we were to do.

That night, at this packed meeting the preacher gave his message and then began to minister to people personally. It wasn't long before this pair of men singled Kitty and I out and began to prophesy: "You are going to minister to people groups and people groups and people groups…" That was interesting to me along with other things that were given to us, which were very powerful and predictive of the world wide ministry that the Father would soon launch us into. Up to this point we saw our ministry as touching lives one at a time not particularly focused on what I considered the "big ticket" issues involving nations and global issues.

A few years later Kitty and I found ourselves traveling the nation having sold out the business and committed ourselves full time to this work that we now do. We were staying for a few weeks in Florida when the phone rang and a lady minister on the other line invited us to speak at a conference of Hispanic churches in West Palm Beach – a few hundred miles away. "I want you to bring the word of the Lord to the Hispanic people…" was the request. My mind instantly when back to the little home meeting in Springfield, Missouri. "You are going to minister to people groups and people groups and people groups…"

In preparing for this conference I asked the Father "how do you minister to a 'people group'?" The Lord replied "the same way you minister to an individual…" I thought about that and while I am not sure I fully understood, I did realize what God was asking me to do. When the time came for us to minister to the several Hispanic churches gathered in this conference the word of the Lord came to us just as it did when we prayed for people one on one.

"The Hispanic people in the earth and specifically in the United States are coming to promotion…"

The word that we then went on to give is that which is included in this book. I understood that the gospel was the gospel to the "nations" and again, in the scriptures that means the "ethnicities". I realizes that addressing ethnic issues was a real minefield that could get me into trouble, but I also knew what God was saying and that this was an important part of our call. The group we met with that day was greatly blessed and encouraged and we have shared the word for the Hispanic people to millions since then on TV networks, Hispanic congregations and many small groups as well. At the end of our time with these lovely Hispanic believers in West Palm Beach we were approached by an African American pastor.

"When will you come and bring the word of the Lord to OUR people?"

I knew it was prophetic. If God would use us to speak to the Hispanic people then no doubt it would be His plan for us to speak the prophetic word to the African peoples specifically in America.

It was then I understood at the next city we travelled to what God had in mind. Our host in Columbia, SC was a beautiful African-American lady who received us into her home and treated us with great care and love. We ministered to several groups in this city and on Sunday our friend took us to a large African American congregation of several thousand of which we were the only white people attending! To top that off it was Black History month! We were immersed into an exposure to Black culture that day that was unforgettable and humbling to us as we witnessed the deep piety of the people, their love for God and for each other. In the midst of this, the deep rumbling of the spirit of God churned up a word in my spirit for the African American people group in our country:

"First in suffering – first in promotion..."

This was a powerful word that we have been able to share with hundreds in the years since then and it is included elsewhere in this book.

In receiving and giving out these words to the Hispanic people and the African American demographic I found it easy because it was a word of consolation and promotion. I was more uneasy, however when pondering the prophetic destiny of the white majority in the Western World. What would God be disposed to say? Would it be a reproof or rebuke? That wasn't in my nature, and my understanding of the prophetic is that God blesses us into a place of correction and not reviling or condemning any people for whom Christ died.

It was months later that after much prayer and seeking God that the message to the white majority of whom I am one began to coalesce in my spirit. We were ministering by coincidence in Northern Ireland and our host (who since has become a respected friend and a member of our board of directors) handed me a book on the history of the Celtic church. I learned that even back as far as the time that Paul was penning his epistles that there were Celtic apostles preaching the gospel in what would become northern England and Northern Ireland. When the Italian church grew to dominate western Europe in the dark ages – the Celtic church for centuries grew and thrived independent of Rome's influence and was of a distinctly different character.

During these centuries, Islam rose in the middle east and scholars and academics fled Egypt and made their way to Northern Ireland seeking a refuge from Islam as far as they could possibly go. Northern Ireland was then, a refuge of the faith and a bastion of learning and academia whose seminal development would influence the world in ways that it would be difficult to exaggerate. In the midst of this the Celtic church thrived. They honored the gifts of the Spirit and believed deeply in an experiential spirituality that was very personal and transcended the mere infrastructure of a religious culture. They were prophetic in nature and they also deeply honored the place of women in the life and leadership of their spiritual communities. They held community bonds that were deeply respected and endeared their children as a gift from God as they nurtured and educated the young in the things of God and in education in general.

The early Celts understood the working of the Holy Spirit as well. They didn't exactly relate to the idea of the Holy Spirit being a "dove" so they adopted the idea of the "Wild Goose of the Holy Ghost", that so typically reflected the character of their own culture and spirituality. Wild geese are very territorial and protective of one another. Wild geese are loud and obnoxious and fiercely loyal to one another. Wild geese in Roman times served as an early warning system against invading armies and as such reflect the deeply prophetic nature of the Celtic peoples toward hearing from God and proclaiming what they heard in secret from the roof tops. When Kitty and I travelled in northern England and Northern Ireland we proclaimed the message of the Wild Goose of the Holy Ghost and the response was amazing! In normally staid and reserved congregations the people responded uproariously, so much so that we were shouted down by the exuberance and rejoicing of a people responding deeply to a message that touched them in ways that resonated to the very depths of their being.

In all of this I saw the answer to the question I had been asking the Father for months. What was the prophetic word to the white demographic in the western world? That word was:

The Wild Goose of the Holy Ghost is Arising Once again in the Earth!

To a person of African descent or Hispanic background this may not have meaning, but for those of us descended from Irish, English and Gallic extraction it is a resonate message of hope, restoration and renewal.

Let me ask you a question: What is the greatness of the white majority historically? Now this is a loaded question, and many scholars and sociologists would be quick to lapse into a focus on the negative, citing the scourge of racism, white privilege and the suppression and brutalization of minority peoples at the hands of predominately white societies – and they would not be wrong. It would be difficult to exaggerate the heartlessness with which white culture has ravaged minority races – all in the name of expansion, economy and pursuit of the perceived manifest destiny of the white demographic. Much of these sins have been perpetrated with the tacit and many times outright approval and endorsement of churchmen, popes and pastors for generations, as bigotry and race hatred has dominated the pulpits of the west. But is that all there is? Of course not. Just as the Father loves and nurtures and has a plan for the Hispanic peoples, and the African peoples he likewise has a redemptive purpose for those of us of white extraction.

The Wild Goose of the Holy is Ghost is Arising Once Again!

As the Hispanic and African peoples come to promotion in the earth what is to be the white response? That of John the Baptist when he spoke of Jesus from beleaguered Galilee. "He must increase but I must decrease..." I submit to you that the fact that white people in the western world are moving into a minority position in their nations, is a sign from God. We are being called once again into a place of being servant sons in the earth to advocate and lift up and serve the impoverished and disenfranchised of the earth. This is where the white races have always shined. In the academic institutions that have made our nations great. In the development of the arts and literature and social sciences. As academics and teachers and facilitators of those rising up to claim their untapped potential.

There are those in the white majority that would bristle at the thought that we as a people are being called to enable and serve those races that are now in God's design coming to majority in our economies and our cultures. I submit to you that if we are the greatest in position before God, it is not because we continue to successfully suppress other races as has been done in times past, but because we choose to SERVE the peoples of the earth, to be servant sons laying down our lives because God has been so good to us as a people and we want to acknowledge in His sovereignty. The fact that the pendulum swings, and now we have the honor of facilitating the same promotion in the minority races who historically have not enjoyed the inherent privilege that has been ours for hundreds of years.

This is a sobering time for white people in the western world. Will we resist the demographic shift that is coming into our culture? Or will we embrace it and ask the Father to make us a part of the solution and not part of the problem? The Father showed me that, as in times of old that Northern England and Northern Ireland will once again become a bastion of culture and learning and community. Out of the halls of academic institutions will come a missional people with the zeal to lay their lives down in service to the nations of the world and will do so in far flung and often dangerous settings in Africa, the Arabian Peninsula and eastern Europe as well. The next 50 years will mark tremendous missionary advances into resistant cultures, bringing not the contaminated message of cultural diversity but the living and breathing message of the Lord Jesus Christ, that will be attended by signs, wonders and the boisterous, joy filled character of the wild goose of the Holy Ghost making Himself known in a radical way that will shift culture and bring the white demographic of the west into a new and honored place of loving service to the peoples of the earth.

CHAPTER 16

A LAND INVASION OF THE U.S.

The Father spoke to me that there will be a land incursion by a foreign power against the mainland of America. This was particularly astonishing, but clearly communicated to me by the Holy Spirit. I saw that this would not result in any strategic overthrow of our country, but that there would be tactical victories that the armed forces would be hard pressed to throw back. How could this be, and how might this happen? The porous borders of the southern states and Mexico were brought to my attention. I was reminded of the prophecies of an obscure Romanian pastor by the name of Dumitru Duduman who foresaw something similar though on a much broader scale.

For me to share with you the vision of the late Dumitru Duduman I must give my caveats to his message. This vision is his own and I would ask that it be judged as simply that and not an extension of what I am giving you from the Father. There have been many prophets over the years – respected ministers who have foreseen land invasions of the United States. George Washington himself while wintering in Valley Forge saw our country defeated by a foreign power. Will this happen? Remember two things: we see through a glass darkly and everything is subject to change. In the book of Jonah, Ninevah was condemned to destruction but the fall of the city never came because they repented. Did this make Jonah a false prophet? No. The purpose of the prophetic word is to avert, not bring judgment. Having said that let us consider the words of Dumitru Duduman and others that have foreseen military calamity come upon our nation. The following is one account of a widely documented vision in which Duduman foresaw the destruction of our nation:

Demetitru Duduman's Vision: (circa 1980's) [source unattributed]

Dumitru Duduman was a Romanian pastor that smuggled bibles into Russia. He was captured and tortured. He was put in the electric chair to die. When he was close to death, Gabriel the archangel appeared to him and he miraculously survived and eventually escaped Romania to the United States. Duduman did not speak English, and much of his message was translated with the help of his young teen-age grandson at the time. Duduman was not a sophisticated person and was very rustic and crude of speech. My suggestion to you is to suspend your skepticism just enough to consider what Duduman was convinced that God had revealed to him:

When he moved to the U.S., Duduman received a vision from the Lord concerning the U.S. and specifically California, Las Vegas, New York, Nevada, and Florida. He was told in an angelic visitation that these cities were as Sodom and Gomorrah and that in one day they would burn. It is interesting that in the intervening years since this vision was given that Florida and California have suffered a dramatic rise of forest fires claiming many lives and hundreds of millions in damages and destruction.

Duduman was told as well that there would be a land invasion of America and in one day it will burn. In one day, Duduman maintained, there will be an attack and the people of the Lord were therefore instructed to flee into the wilderness to escape from sudden destruction that would come. The nations that were foreseen to attack were Russia, Cuba, Nicaragua, Mexico, and 2 others that where forgotten by Duduman.

In Duduman's own words:

It was late at night and I was sitting outside my home on a rock. A light came toward me. The fear of cars came with me. The Romanian Police tried to run over me with cars. That's why I jumped up. The light surrounded me. Out of the light I heard the same voice. It said, "Dumitru, why are you so despaired?"

I said, "Why did you punish me? What did I do that was so rotten that you brought me to the United States? I have nowhere to lie my head down upon. I can't understand anybody."

He said, "Dumitru, didn't I tell you that I am here with you also? I brought you here to this country because this country will burn."

"Then why did you bring me here to burn? Why didn't you let me die in my own country?"

"Dumitru, have patience and I will tell you. Get beside me."

I don't know what it was. Brothers, I got beside the angel. He showed me all of California. He showed me all the cities of California. Then he showed me Las Vegas.

"You see what I have shown you? This is Sodom and Gomorrah. In one day it will burn."

He said, "It's sin has reached the Holy One."

He showed me another great city. He said, "Do you know what city this is?"

I said, "No."

He said, "This is New York City. This is Sodom and Gomorrah. In one day it will burn."

He showed me Florida. He said, "This is Florida. This is Sodom and Gomorrah. In one day it will burn."

He didn't let me say a word until he brought me back to the place we had left. He said, "Now, Dumitru, you can ask me questions."

He said, "I brought you to this country. Dumitru, I want to wake up a lot of people. I love this country. I love the people. I want to save them. America will burn."

I said, "How can I save them? I can't even speak their language. Who knows me here? How will they call me?"

He said, "Don't worry. I will be ahead of you. I will make great healings among the American people. You will go to television stations, radio stations and churches. Tell them everything I tell you. Don't hide anything. If you try to hide anything I will punish you. America will burn."

"How will America burn? It is so powerful."

He said, "The Russian spies have discovered where the most powerful nuclear missiles are in America. It will start with the world calling for 'peace, peace'. Then there will be an internal revolution in America, started by the Communists. The government will be busy with internal problems. Then, from the oceans, Russia, Cuba, Nicaragua, Central America, Mexico, and two other countries (which I cannot remember) will attack! The Russians will bombard the nuclear missile silos in America. America will burn.

I said, "What will you do with the church?"

He said, "The church has left me."

I said, "How? Don't you have people here?"

He said, "People in America honor people. The honor that should be given to God, they give to other people. Americans think highly of themselves. They say, 'I serve God,' but they don't. In the church there is divorce, adultery, fornication, sodomy, abortion and all kinds of sin. Jesus Christ doesn't live in sin. He lives in holiness. I brought you here so you could cry out loud. Don't be afraid. I am with you. Tell them to stop sinning. God never stops forgiving. Tell them to repent. He will forgive them. Tell them to start preparing themselves so I can save them in the day of trouble."

The angel went on to tell Duduman what to instruct God's people regarding what was coming:

I said, "How will you save the Church if America will burn?"

He said, "Tell them as I tell you. As he saved the three young men through the oven of fire, and Daniel from the mouth of the lion, that is how I will save them. Tell them to stop sinning and repent.

"I have blessed this country because of the Jews that are here. I have 7 million Jews here. They haven't tasted war or persecution. God blessed them more than anyone else. Instead of thanking God, they started sinning and doing wickedly. Their sins have reached the Holy one. God will punish them with fire. Israel doesn't recognize the Messiah, because they place their trust on the power of the Jews in America. When God will hit America, all the nations will be terrified.

"God will raise up China, Japan and many other nations and they will beat the Russians. They will push them back to the gates of Paris. There they will make a peace treaty, but they will make the Russians their leader. All the nations with the Russians as their leader go against Israel. It's not that they want to. God makes them.

Israel doesn't have the help of the Jews in America anymore. In their terror, when they see what is coming, they will call upon the Messiah. The Messiah will come to help Israel. Then the church of God will meet Him in the clouds (1 Thes.4:16).

Are you ready to meet Jesus Christ? Are your wedding clothes clean? If there are still spots on the clothes of your soul, then the blood of Jesus Christ still has power to cleanse sins. Jesus Christ will live with the Church on the Mount of Olives. He himself will fight against the nations.

I said, "If you are the angel of God, everything you tell me has to be written in the Bible. If it is not, then I can't tell the Americans."

"Tell them to read Jeremiah 51:8-15. He names it 'The Mystery Babylon, The Great Adulteress.' Also, Revelation Chapter 18, the entire chapter. There it says clearly what will happen to America."

Why did he name it, "The Mystery Babylon"?

"Tell them because all the nations of the world immigrated into America and America accepted them. America accepted Buddha, the devil church, the sodomite church, the Mormon church and all kinds of wickedness. America was a Christian nation. Instead of stopping them, they went after their gods. Because of this, He named them "The Mystery Babylon."

When we read such things we may be astonished into complete unbelief and rejection of such a vision. I would go further and inform you that George Washington himself saw a complete military overthrow of our country out of which we would rise from the ashes to form a new and powerful nation state in the aftermath of a global conflict. Space does not allow for the inclusion of Washington's vision but it is reminiscent as well to visions given to the late A.A. Allen, David Wilkerson and to some degree as well, the late John Paul Jackson.

What do we make of such things? In speaking of the last days Jesus made the following statement in the gospel of Matthew:

[Mat 24:6 KJV] 6 And ye shall hear of wars and rumours of wars: see that ye be not troubled: for all [these things] must come to pass, but the end is not yet.

Nations rise and nations fall. Would God allow America to fall? In the vision the Father gave me this was not the overthrow of our nation. This was a small scale invasion that would be so swift and brutal that our armed forces spread across the globe and stretched to their limit would have great difficulty in repelling but would repel nonetheless. Where would this take place? Duduman foresaw part of the invasion in his vision coming to the San Diego area. In the vision the Father gave me I saw extreme southern California as the target of this incursion. The attack will come and the military will struggle to promptly respond, but respond they will and the enemy will be thrown back. Duduman's prophesy if it comes to pass at all will not be in the next 50 years but there will be a definite and startling attack on the mainland of the U.S. that will underscore and foment among our citizens an insecurity about just how safe we are in our own borders.

What can we conclude from this? First of all, and to state again "the sky isn't falling the kingdom is coming..." Whether our nation faces an invasion or internal pressures that break up the Union, God is still on the throne. In the early centuries of the church the people of God were spread across the Middle East and

Europe and endured much upheaval of a very severe nature - yet the church survived, thrived and conquered. Would God allow the US to fall? Any serious student of eschatology and the end times would admit that there is no indication that the US figures prominently in end time events just before the return of Christ. Whether our nation ceases to exist or is simply marginalized on the world stage by no longer being the superpower it once was – change is upon us.

St. Augustine in his classic work "City of God" stated that God is not inherently committed to any one nation or any one form of government. God is not a capitalist. He is not committed to an inviolate protection of the representative governments of the west including the US. Augustine declared that the value of any nation or government is found only in the manner and scope by which it facilitates the spread of the gospel. In the US and in the UK, the assault on faith and suppression of faith is becoming more and more painfully clear. We could push the panic button and join the conspiracy theorists of our day or we can simply continue to trust in the living God as the church of the first three centuries did and who eventually overthrew the might of Rome and established rule in the earth across the known world through the religious adherence of the Caesars whether out of political expediency or otherwise, it was the hand of God that raised them up and the hand of God that brought Rome down in the furtherance of the purposes of the kingdom.

Change is at hand. Change is upon us. We are not to fret, however or to become insurgent in our character or activist in our agenda, as the church of the living God. Before we are citizens of earth we are citizens in heaven. We do not serve God at the indulgence of secular rule. The kings of the earth rule at the indulgence and tolerance of our heavenly Father and He will always be in the midst of whatever world events may look like – to defend and protect the people of God.

CHAPTER 17
REVIVAL IN EUROPE

A few years ago the Father spoke to me about going to Europe and to the UK on apostolic assignment. My wife and I had visited Royal Gorge in Colorado on vacation and were driving back by car. It was a beautiful day and as we drove along we were enjoying what my wife calls "windshield time". All the distractions of the cell phone and the office were set aside and we could enjoy each other and commune with God as the miles rolled by. We know what it is to be travelling along and have Jesus come alongside and go with us as He did the two on the road to Emmaus. Many times our hearts have burned within us as He began to talk and reveal Himself, making Himself and His plans for us known on these extended road trips. We have put 10's of 1000's of miles on our vehicle in travelling for the ministry and the road time was never wasted because the Holy Spirit was present ministering to us, encouraging us and instructing us.

After coming through the mountains and down through the city of Denver, we were making our way across eastern Kansas. Kitty was dozing in the passenger seat and as I drove the Lord began to speak to me. He said "next year you will travel to 12 major cities in the US". I thought OK! That sounds great, Lord! In reality in the following year we crossed the US 4 times by car and ministered in 166 cities, turning down 125 invitations on what became known as the "Jericho Drive". We committed wholesale to what God told us to do – even vacating the home we were renting and giving away all of our possessions except what we needed in the car for our travels. We know what it is to "give all" and "sell all" in obedience to a mandate from heaven. A few years before I had given a prophecy about "sell all, give all" as Jesus said and I heard my mouth say "it isn't about impoverishment – it's about empowerment to serve!" I knew at the time that the word wasn't for the group in front of us but it was for us, and we walked it out with great victory because we heard what God said and did it no matter what the cost!

After telling us we were going to go into the nation we further heard the Father say that we would go to 12 countries. After completing the "Jericho Drive" and holding a "Shout the Shout" conference in Branson, Missouri we made plans to leave for Europe to obey the mandate of heaven. We did all this by the leading of the Holy Spirit. We didn't get on the phone to generate meeting dates or financial support. We went out ASKING NOTHING or PLANNING ANYTHING, and God met us in the way and prospered us throughout Europe as we ministered and prophesied and brought the word of the Lord to a hungry and passionate people.

When we were in London our meetings were packed and the people were jubilant and hungry for the prophetic word. In the hotel during the day we took over the pub, meeting with pastors and leaders, prophesying into their lives and speaking to their destinies. The hunger was palpable and the favor of God gave us strength and vitality to minister in back to back one-on-one sessions, small groups and larger meetings. When we made our way to Barnard Castle in northern England we connected with Prophet Eunice Brennan and she was a real gate opener to the area. We continued with ongoing one-on-one meetings, small groups and a larger meeting in the backroom of a church on the main street of this small town. The room was packed and we spoke of the "Wild

Goose of the Holy Ghost" that was ascending again upon the land of the ancient Celts. The room erupted and I couldn't even finish my sentences. The people stood up and ran. They fell on the floor. They shouted. They laughed. They cried. They rejoiced. God was in the house!

As we ministered the Father gave a word that has implications not only for Eunice and her leadership or just for Barnard Castle but for all of England, northern and southern and for Northern Ireland as well:

The Father says that Barnard Castle is as Hernhut (where the Moravian movement was birthed). Herrnhut means "the Lord's Watchful care". The Father says I have watched over England and I have watched over Ireland, and I am bringing an unprecedented outpouring of My Spirit that will not fail and will not be contemned.

The Father says over Northern England and Northern Ireland that I am bringing up four prophetic influencers to breathe My wind into the flames of revival in the United Kingdom. There will be four prophetic influencers who by their association to one another will spawn a prophetic community, they will participate in raising up in northern England a relevant prophetic culture. This prophetic generation will inspire, guide, and commission a wave of missional passion that will retrace many of the steps of British missionaries of old. These missionaries will go forth with the sponsorship of the Holy Ghost against a wave of persecution and criticism from organized religion.

There is coming a great outpouring the Spirit of God to the UK and Southern Europe. The enemy is working overtime to close the borders and cast a net of fear and futility over the nations of western Europe but this will come to failure. The seeds of fidelity and revival planted decades and even centuries ago are still thriving and about to break through the resistance of nations long hardened against the claims of Christ. The blood of the martyrs is crying out to the throne of God from years past that they might see the travail of their souls and be satisfied that the lives they sold cheap into the gospel will receive the manifestation and answer for their prayers of revival outpouring in the streets of cities throughout western Europe.

In London, the spirit of heaviness and futility is being lifted. A new joy is coming to Londoners as a wave of love and hope and expectation is coming to turn the hearts of the people again to the rock that bore them. Years ago I heard the cry of God over the city of London. It was a cry to the men and women of God who sigh and cry because of the abominations and secularism that has plowed under religious expression in the United Kingdom. I heard the Spirit of God call out to Londoners to "man the barricades of love…" To my sisters and brothers in the UK I say to you that politics will not save you. Economic reforms will not save you. Withdrawing from the EU is not the solution. I am bringing says the Father an outpouring of My love that will wash away the filth of your city and restore again the ancient pathways.

At this point I inform the reader that the Spirit of Prophecy compels me with the strength of this word to speak it in the "first person prophetic":

Make it your determination says the Father to the citizens of London and to the faithful in Christ to give yourselves over to My love. Receive My love and share My love with all those that you find around you. Go out and make eye contact in the streets and in the subways. Let My love and My Spirit shine out through you and you will be amazed even as Muslims and unbelievers will begin to flock to you. As you give yourself to your city, as I gave Myself to Jerusalem you will see change come. Love never fails says the Father. I am calling you to man the barricades of Love. The tide of ungodliness that is rushing in great waves over your city and your nation will be held back and turned back not by political activism or strident activist preaching. It is My love. My love will turn the tide. My love will be the barrier that will stop the enemy in his tracks.

As you go out and love the unlovely you will see bombers and terrorists because of love, who will turn themselves in and confess in contrition and repentance. Mark My words says the Father you will see this with your eyes and hear it with your ears. The eyes of the world will look on this stunning event and every ear will tingle. The enemy will fear and the pundits will howl – they will suggest that some new Christian sect is rising in the boroughs of London that is worse than Islam! My love flowing through you will terrorize the forces of secularism. Just keep loving. Just keep loving and laughing says the Father for I am not done with London and I will not be denied in My great purposes with what I have started in the United Kingdom – I will surely finish.

The missional fervor of Northern Ireland and northern England is spilling over into London and southern Europe. I am raising up a prophetic people from the rural areas west of Belfast and they will come. They will come as apostolic reformers and prophetic voices that will be heard and will not be denied. They will speak of the ancient ways of the Celtic saints and the New Age movement that has contaminated the public personae of the great English people will be wholly purged from their hearts. They will turn at the preaching of those who come from Barnard and Manchester and New Castle on Tyne. The old rivalries and hatreds among My people in England and Ireland will die in the deluge of love and My glory that is coming upon the United Kingdom. The Wild Goose of the Holy Ghost is arising and she will bring a wind of revival over the land that will invade even the royal family and for the first time in centuries a piety and passion for the living Christ will be known among the royals that will wholly scandalize those who think such things are bad form and poor public policy.

I am bringing a change says the Father and you are a participator in it. The Father says to the city of London and to My people therein that an outpouring is at hand. It has already begun.

So GET READY says the Father for I choose you! I choose those in obscure places to come forth and band together in a apostolic community across the UK to defy the principalities and powers of secularism and see a new Great Awakening reshape this nation and restore the testimony of those who were planted in faith after lives lived in missional sacrifice to bring the gospel around the world. The day will come that the empire I raise up in the United Kingdom will not be the empire of man but a spiritual dominion that will bring the gospel to the nations that will not be condemned or suppressed or stymied. I choose you says the Father because you made yourselves available to Me in an unprecedented way. I will make you and I will take you and I will spend you for My kingdom until all the nations of the earth resound with a fresh testimony and demonstration of My greatness flowing from the great nations represented by the United Kingdom!

CHAPTER 18
PAYMENT OF AFRICA'S LOVE DEBT TO THE UK

Arriving in Heathrow for the first time overseas, I was struck with the well-ordered environment at the airport and the cleanliness of the area where entry and customs was conducted for foreign visitors. Being 53 years of age at the time, I had never travelled out of the country and viewed everything with wide-eyed wonder. Since the inception of our ministry God had launched us out of the business world and the brick and mortar pulpit ministry and sent us across the US from coast to coast. In 2013 alone we traversed the US four times conducting prophetic meetings and introducing people to the idea that God calls prophets today and everyone should know who the prophet is in their life. The challenge was always "if you don't know – it's because you don't have one – and how's that working for you?" Our ministry from the beginning was one mandated to be an advocate for the prophetic even though at that time the idea of being a prophet was still gaining on our own thinking about our specific calls – even though we prophesied daily to many 100's of people in a year.

In 2012 when the Father told us we would go coast to coast and minister in 12 major areas of the US, He also told us we would go overseas. We knew that the UK would be our first stop. During the course of May 2014 we hopped on 10 flights crisscrossing Western Europe – but mainly focusing on London, Northern Ireland and northern England, specifically the Durham area and Barnard Castle, where one of our prophetic interns lived. When we first accepted the fact that we were tasked by the Father to go overseas the first thing we had to do was get passports. That took a while because we had no idea where to get a passport or what was expected from us by the government to be willing to issue us one. The second thing we had to determine was exactly HOW does one go to the UK or other countries in Europe? Did we have to have permission ahead of time? Did we need a written approval or permit in order to board a plane bound for Heathrow? We had no clue. We talked to many of our friends and mentors who were involved in overseas ministry and most of them strangely were no help because our questions apparently were so simple they didn't make sense to those world travelers we knew, who went overseas all the time.

Thank God we have a dear friend, Pam Rice who has in her lifetime travelled the world extensively both for personal, business and ministry reasons. She was a part of the leadership of the Vineyard movement at its height and her involvement and participation in this worldwide phenomena in the 80's and 90's uniquely qualified her to counsel us in our ignorance regarding just how to BE a globetrotting pair of ministers. Pam's experience at being a part of such a large ministry has been of great value to us as we have come from very meager beginnings and encountered many new things that the voice of an experienced veteran such as Pam could assist and help us with. Because of this and her friendship with us personally we nominated her to sit on the board of directors of Father's Heart Ministry, as a valued influence and leadership to the things God has called us to do that are so in common with that which she has already done. Many times Pam will pick up the phone when we are traveling or planning a conference and share her wisdom – knowing without asking exactly where we are in our thinking and just what wisdom would be of benefit to us.

On this particular trip we arrived at Heathrow very late in the evening. We took a cab to the Lancaster Gate Hotel and settled in for the night. The next day we went down to breakfast. The first thing I noticed was the ethnic diversity among the people serving and those enjoying the breakfast buffet. There were actually very few Anglo's in the crowd which surprised me. As a Midwesterner I had a certain presupposition of what the make-up of the people would be in urban London, and quite honestly I had it all wrong. The majority of the people were non-white. These included African immigrants, Indians, Pakistanis and Asians, but for the most part black people of African nationality who had immigrated to the UK seeking the economic opportunity to be found there.

The accents of the English speaking people were impressive to us, since our experience was limited to American accents from various parts of the US. In our naiveté every English speaking person with their variations of English accents sounded so pleasant and unique, it was a joy just to hear them speak. Even the breakfast was an adventure. An English breakfast includes things such as (what we call) pork and beans and something called black pudding.

Many of our ministry friends and followers were aware that we had arrived and we conducted 2 larger meetings and scores of one on one meetings with those in London who loved our anointing and desired to be ministered to prophetically. We conducted these sessions at a table in a pub in the hotel and in a side room to the conference room we used for our larger meeting. There were all ethnicities represented but the majority were black people mostly from Africa but many from the Caribbean as well.

As we ministered to each person, couple or family in turn, the spirit of prophecy moved strongly upon us as we spoke into the potential of each person. The passion for Christ was palpable in the hearts of these beautiful ebony skinned believers. They shook.

They wept. They swooned under the anointing. They shouted and spoke ecstatic utterances. All the while we were prophesying over them for a total of 6 days in London in 3 different locations. As we spoke by the spirit of Prophecy I was struck with the awesome and very moving passion in these people's hearts. As I thought on these things I realized that almost all of them came generationally from family lines that at one time were living in paganism and shamanism knowing nothing of Christ. It was ironic in a sacred kind of way that these people who had streamed to the United Kingdom to seek their fortunes and follow God's plan for their lives, originally had no doubt for the most part been evangelized by English missionaries during a time when sun never set on the British Empire.

During these ministry days in London the Father spoke to me in the strongest of terms that *"the continent of Africa would pay it's love debt to the United Kingdom…"*

Now before I proceed further let me first recognize the fact that the exploitation of the African peoples by the English speaking world does not escape my attention, and if you are reading this chapter before all others perhaps you might peruse the chapters dealing with the "first in suffering – first in promotion" message to the black race in a previous chapter. The gospel according to Jesus is the gospel to the "nations" and the word "nations" in the New Testament speaks most prominently of ETHNICITIES which include black, white, Asian and so forth. It is a political and cultural minefield then, to faithfully give the word of God out to the people in the context it was intended in an ethnic framework. However, we cannot and will not ignore the powerful truths and blessings that God gives looking upon not only individuals but on people groups and ethnics groups.

At the commencement of the 1800's Christianity was very little in evidence on the continent of Africa outside of Ethiopia and the vestiges of the Kongolese Empire. History does record early

Catholic missionaries and Protestants as well but Missional campaigns did not reach a full on pitch until the time that slavery was abolished from 1807 to 1834. The great David Livingstone was a trail blazer in missionary efforts having great success not so much in his direct missionary activity (other than in modern day Botswana), but in advocating colonization of the continent which over time opened the floodgates for waves of missionary workers from the British empire to Africa, spreading the gospel of Jesus Christ. British missionaries and other European missionaries laid their lives down to the task of gospel work among the peoples of Africa with great success in the 1800's. There were abuses to be sure but the fact of the matter is, that it was the British empire and missionaries in coming in the spirit of David Livingstone over many decades who poured their life out like a drink offering upon African soil. To such selfless servants the peoples of Africa owe a great love debt to the now tepid and lukewarm remnants of the British and European churches who originally sponsored the work of these tireless missionaries that so transformed their continent.

In 2013 as Kitty and I travelled throughout the UK we particularly saw in the streets of London so many Africans and peoples originating from the African continent. Indeed, we really didn't make very many powerful connections with Anglo believers until we made our way to the north of England outside the urban setting of London. But oh, what a zeal we saw among the immigrant population of London. The believers there demonstrated a hunger for God, and maturity in spiritual things that could only be paralleled by the sacred history of communities such as the Antioch church and the Ephesian church of the first century. I asked the Father "what are you doing in bringing so many Christians into this country through the immigration process – particularly from the African continent?"

The Father answered me with great clarity – reminding me of the history that I have duplicated here of Livingstone, and the wave of British and European missionaries who sold their lives cheap into the work of the gospel in behalf of the peoples of the African continent. Surely it is no exaggeration that while the other continents of the world are seeing a sharp decline of Christian Culture – that African Christianity whose foundation was laid by these great European and British adventurers in Christ is on the up rise.

To that the Father has sovereignly opened the flood gates of European and UK immigration policy to bring now the zealots of Christ from the spiritual children generationally of what was originally a European and British missions effort over 100 years ago – back to the land of Livingstone to pay the love debt in a mighty move of God. This new awakening will be manned and led by anointed men and women of African descent to likewise lay their lives down in service to Christ to the very men and women of the United Kingdom whose culture has in large degree lost its gospel footing!

CHAPTER 19

RADICAL SPIRITUAL SHIFT IN THE US AND EUROPE

The 24 things that God spoke to me would come over the next 50 years were given in the summer of 2015. In the time that has transpired much of what the Father revealed is already coming to pass. The Republican party is in the throes of great upheaval as establishment politicians are losing their hold on the electorate. The Yellowstone caldera is in the news as it is becoming more active than at other times. France and Belgium are in chaos as they prove themselves unable to hold back the scourge of terrorism from their borders.

The Father told me that the US, France and Belgium would be brought to their knees at the foot of the cross. What does this mean? We must look back in history to the beginning centuries of the church. For the first three centuries of the church, persecution and oppression of our fledgling faith was brutal and widespread. In the coliseums and palisades of the Roman empire, the blood of Christians stained the walls as the public shouted "away with the atheists!". The early church was not persecuted because of what they believed but because of what they DIDN'T believe. They believed in only one true God and by extrapolation that conviction nullified the pagan beliefs of those around them. Thus they were seen as a danger to the status quo and were dragged to the stake for execution.

For the church to be so brutally suppressed one wonders how things ever changed? How did this despised Jewish sect grow to a force that overthrew Rome by its piety, to become the foundation upon which the modern world was established? The answer is simple – by how they prayed and how they died. One official, writing to Rome expressed dismay that for every Christian that died in the coliseum there were many that sprang up in his place. "We have to quit killing Christians!" was the frustrated plea to Rome. Yet the deaths and the persecution continued, as did the patience of the saints, and the prayers of the saints. In time, the day came that Christianity became the recognized religion of the realm, and new era began (for better or worse as history shows that Rome was defeated and Christ was exalted nonetheless).

When traveling to France, one encounters a stark gray wall of secularism that has no tolerance for men and women of faith. It is plain and very apparent when walking the streets of Paris, the disdain and spirit of secularism that has plowed under the tender shoots of the faith from centuries past. When a nation forgets its God then consequences are unavoidable. We have seen this in 911, and in the terrible events in France and Belgium in 2016. Years ago when the Berlin wall came down, I asked the Lord what this meant – because natural boundaries also represent spiritual boundaries. He told me that the western world was no longer safe from terrorism. He told me terrorism would come to American shores. Shortly thereafter, the bombing in Oklahoma City shattered the peace of our country and that was only the beginning of what was coming. The same is true for France and for Belgium.

Terrorism is on the rise. Al Qaeda has weakened, only to be replaced by a much more virulent strain of terror in the form of ISIS. When ISIS is marginalized there will be another Jihad and another and another as the western world grapples with the reality of the age of social media and the existence of porous borders within which no government or people are safe from the detonation of a bomb or the fanatical fatalism of a suicidal Jihadist. In the coming half century terrorism will continue to bleed the US, France and Belgium. There will be no answers. Politics, governments and militaries will spend billions of dollars and lay claim to many successes but the situation will continue. Why? Because the word of God cannot be broken:

> [Psa 9:17 KJV] 17 *The wicked shall be turned into hell, [and] all the nations that forget God.*

Our nations and their governments are corrupt and spiritually contaminated from the top down. As Isaiah said *"the whole head is sick – the whole heart is faint"*. Because of this, consequences are unavoidable. Why? Because God hates us? No. God respects free will. He will not turn humanity into a race of automatons who cannot but worship before his throne as mere drones – intoning their reverence in monotonous religious drivel. On the contrary God gives us free will. With free will there must be the consequences that proceed from the choices that individuals, ethnicities and nations make. The US, France and Belgium are in a reaping season. For two centuries the tide of secularism has swept the honor of God and country from the minds of the public replacing it with a God-rejecting subjectivism that only celebrates the fullest extent of debauchery and rebellion that man can conjure up. The harvest of those bitter seeds is come to maturity in the unstoppable tide of Jihad across our borders. Our nations have despised and hated all things religious, or having to do with God and are now helpless to defend themselves against a religion of hatred whose scorn for the western world is only matched by the western world's scorn and hatred for the God of their forefathers.

The US, France and Belgium will be brought to their knees. The governments that cannot protect their populations are increasingly falling out of favor. There is now a sweeping movement in these nations to reject incumbent leaders and elect reform candidates. Within three election cycles it will become apparent that the reform candidates and their political platforms have no answers either. The public will be casting about for some hope or some glimmer of light to lead them out of the darkness, chaos and fear that will continue to grip the world. Suicide rates will soar. Consumer based economy will fall under the weight of their own excesses, hedonism and capitalism. Economies will be crushed by the unchecked appetites of a terrified people bankrupting themselves with materialism vainly seeking to avoid looking at the bleak world outlook before them.

Many in the coming years will resort to false religions. Sexual cults will arise that will blend pseudo shamanism with a new form of Satanism – practicing openly every form of debauchery known to exist in our society. Institutional religions will shutter their doors as they no longer have the adherents in sufficient numbers to continue their activities. The bleakness of the world outlook will be suffocating in the US, UK, France and Belgium as wave after wave of economic struggle, terrorism and political scandal rock the populations of these nations and turn them darkly pessimistic.

And then God. In the midst of scandal, darkness and chaos there is arising in the US, UK, France and Belgium a generation of young reformers who will at a grass roots level begin to transform and bring the light of God to their age groups. Revival fires will ignite and even the streets of Paris will be filled with young men and young women passionate for Christ parading their faith without fear before the jackbooted militarism of a modern police force designed to defeat Jihad - but now turning against their own young people. In Belgium commerce and traffic will grind to a halt and young men and women take to the streets in an Occupy style uprising not calling for economic reform but for joyful repentance and acknowledgment of the living God. The older generation – the 60's generation will look on in horror as the faith they have worked so hard to stamp out springs to vibrancy and life in the hearts of their children and their grandchildren.

On the capital mall in Washington DC, a throng of 10's of 1000's of young people will gather from the east coast and the west coast to call for repentance and revival in our land. They will refuse to disband. They will challenge law enforcement to take them to prison, to launch their tear gas to disperse them. They will not be throwing bottles or Molotov cocktails – they will be giving hugs and laying their lives down on bended knee proclaiming the love of Christ. In this generation of young people, a confrontation of secularism will be confronted on a scale unprecedented in 200 years. They will not be reasoned with. They will not respond to threats. They will not be manipulated. They will declare the pure gospel of the Lord Jesus Christ in a manner that will confront nations. They will not be marginalized and they will not be ignored and their testimony will be Christ and Him Crucified.

CHAPTER 20
ISLAM WILL BE MARGINALIZED

What is the future of Jihad? Will terrorism go unchecked in the indeterminate future? Is there no end? Governments and military strategists struggle to overcome and deal with the low-tech, low profile nature of terrorism in the modern world. Where did all of this come from? What we are really dealing with is a variation of guerilla warfare directed at the civilian population. The civilian populations are targeted because in the representative governments of the west, the resolve of heads of state and armies is measured in the patience of the people. The endurance of an nations electorate wears thin tolerating the often meddlesome foreign policy of any government that brings down death and destruction on the heads of an otherwise peaceful rank and file.

Where did the idea of guerilla warfare / terrorism come from in the modern world? The most influential example we can give in recent history is the Vietnam war. Our country went to war with a small, impoverished Indonesian country and were soundly beaten by a brutal war of attrition that has left a lasting scar on the psyche of the American people. When Nixon declared he would bomb North Vietnam back to the stone age he didn't take into account that the Vietnamese people were already living not much above an Iron age subsistence as it was.

Where did the Vietnamese learn the guerrilla warfare that was so effective against American troops? Strangely enough – they learned primarily from the Allied Forces during WWII. Eisenhower wanted the indigenous peoples of Indochina to execute an insurgency against the invading Japanese, and provided the incentive and the training to bring this about. One of these insurgent leaders was Ho Chi Min – the leader of the Communist revolution (later on) in Vietnam. When Ho Chi Min was part of the training of the Viet people to bring insurgency against the Japanese, there were promises made of independence from colonial French rule. The fact of the matter was that Ho Chi Min was not always anti-American in his sentiments. At one point Ho petitioned his Allied handlers to allow Viet representatives to stand before the US legislature to make a bid for statehood for a unified Vietnam. These petitions were pandered to and false promises made by the west.

After the war when colonial French rule was reinstated and the people of Vietnam were therefore betrayed. This led to the revolt of Vietnam using the very tactics and materiel provided by the west to resist the Japanese just a few years earlier. The resulting insurgency was one as well that used the very tactics of guerilla warfare and terrorism that are splashed on the news screens every day in the modern world.

French colonialism was brought to its end at the massacre at Dien Ben Fu. What happened next? In steps the United States – to clean up the mess that it had been a part of making when false promises were made to the Viet people. The independence that the Allies in WWII promised the Viet people from French Colonialism they would now take by force. This was all but inevitable. The law of sowing and reaping is unavoidable. What the Allied forces in the Pacific theater (and the United States in particular) – sowed into Indochina with false promises and manipulation was reaped in years of death and bloodshed against an insurgency originally trained and equipped by the US for the purpose of using the Viet people as a proxy resistance against the Japanese.

Over and over this pattern of cold-war imperialism has been repeated in the United States. The reaping that came with the whirlwind traces back to policies of the United states that inevitably brought on devastation against our forces who paid with the blood of our boys on the battlefields of the world. Case in point – when I was inducted into the Air Force in 1978 and mustered into training at Lackland air force base – I was in for a surprise! My flight of 100 American airmen were only one of a few hundred Americans training on one of the largest military installations in the state. There were few Americans, however there were 10's of 1000's of Iraqis training under American handlers to serve in the brutal dictatorship of Sadaam Hussien.

You may remember that this was during the Iran hostage crisis, when in another debacle fueled by the tone deaf foreign policy of the US toward Iran – we backed the Shah who brutalized his people and set the Iranian population on a collision course with the Ayatollahs. While I was in the military I remember when it was reported on the news that Sadaam used US produced mustard gas and phosgene against the Iranian forces on the Iraqi border. The people of the US cheered as the shame of the hostage crises was ameliorated by the brutal tactics of a dictator we saw as the hand of American justice – Sadaam Hussien! I remember that in the early 80's the opening credits of CNN included images of then Vice-President Bush grinning from ear to ear shaking hands with Hussein as our friend and ally. What is wrong with this picture? The despicable nature of American collusion through errant foreign policy can only be measured in the number of deaths both civilian and military. The decision to invade Iraq was necessitated by the ill-advised foreign policy from years before to prop up a dictator we now shed the blood of our boys to depose.

Not surprisingly when allied and coalition forces came to the Arabian Peninsula our enemies needed only look to the stellar example of American defeat in Indochina to decide how best to proceed. The tactics of Jihad, terrorism and guerilla warfare against our modern armies has been very effective and very, very hard to curtail let along bring to a stop. So back to the original question at the beginning of this chapter – is there no end to Jihad? We have already seen the beginning of the end as Al Qaeda and other terrorist organizations in vying for attention on the world scene have turned against each other. In short, the Father is doing in the earth what the nations and armies of the west could not do. Jihad will fall – not because of a coalition victory (though they will take the credit) but because God will cause them to turn against one another as happened time and time again with ancient armies in bible times, who came against God's people and were turned back and defeat in self destructive confusion by the hand of God.

There will be relief from terrorism in the coming years but not because of some wonderful solution cooked up in a bunker or military complex. God will turn the Jihadist dominated countries of the Arabian Peninsula and north Africa in to total barbarianism and anarchy. They will war against one another as an astonished western world looks on. The UK and the US and even the UN will take credit and claim this as a byproduct of master statesmanship but the fact is – it will be the hand of God acting in mercy to alleviate and largely remove the terrorist threat from the homelands of the western world in the next 50 years.

CHAPTER 21
A COMPREHENSIVE OVERVIEW

In August of 2015 when this vision was given to me. it was rapid fire over the course of a church service where Apostle Warren Hunter was preaching. I didn't have a pen and paper so I took out my iPhone and typed out on the small keyboard what the Father was saying. In addition to the 20 predictions mentioned and covered already there were four additional events that the Father spoke to me. The list, in its entirety is largely repeated here from what we have already covered and those remaining events:

One: The Republican Party will be chastised for making merchandise of the Church.

Two: A Liberal Woman will come to power as the President of the United States.

Three: A Homosexual President will sit in the Oval Office

Four: The Church will experience a "Great Disillusionment".

Five: An Unprecedented Prayer Movement will sweep through the Church.

Six: A Great Awakening Will Come.

Seven: A New Evangelical Movement will be born.

Eight: Young Arabic Apostles will come to the Western World.

Nine: Ethnic Justice will come into the Earth.

Ten: The Union will be Threatened by a Sweeping Secessionist Movement.

Eleven: A Great Natural Disaster will come to the US.

Twelve: There will be a Major Eruption of the Yellowstone Caldera.

Thirteen: A Land invasion of the US will be Unsuccessful.

Fourteen: The UK and Europe will see a Great Revival.

Fifteen: Africa will pay its Love Debt to the United Kingdom.

Sixteen: The African American peoples will come to promotion.

Seventeen: The Hispanic peoples will come into the Majority in the USA.

Eighteen: A Generation of Servant Sons will Emerge Out of the ranks of White Privilege.

Nineteen: Secularism in the US, the UK and France will be brought to its knees.

Twenty: Radical Islam will be Marginalized.

Twenty-One: The US and Russia will become the Petro-Center of the Earth.

Twenty-Two: A Revival of Prophetic Ministry will be Headquartered in Helsinki, Finland.

Twenty-Three: Antarctica will become an International Guantanamo – in Fact it Already is.

Twenty-Four: A Republican Senator will be Assassinated – the Spouse of this Legislator will be the First Conservative Woman to take the White House.

The remaining four events (not covered previously) touch on geo-political events in the Arabian Peninsula. When rising oil prices pushed the average price of oil per barrel above $100 a barrel – it made the shale deposits of North America and the oil reserves in Russia viably competitive with the OPEC nations. The attempt of Saudi Arabia and other OPEC nations to economically starve the western based shale-oil companies out of business will fail. It will become necessary for nations in the oil rich Arabian Peninsula to allow oil prices to rise from historic lows in an attempt to stabilize the oil market due to spreading civil war and anarchy in the near east. The Saudi family will be severely weakened by internal strife and will struggle to stay in power as a Shiite minority shifts into a strategy of radicalism aimed directly at toppling the Saudi royal family.

The unrest in the middle east will continue as tourism based economies such as Egypt and Israel will become debtor states that western powers will be forced to prop up in order to avoid further escalations of tensions in the area. The dearth of tourism that has crippled the Egyptian economy will continue to spill over into Israel. Western vacationers will not desire to risk their safety due to increasing instability in the region. The walls and other measures that Israel has enacted to preserve her stability will yield decreasing benefits as desperate Palestinian factions using new technologies will breach those impediments to wreak havoc and bloodshed on the streets of Tel Aviv and the old city of Jerusalem. There will be a major terrorist attack at the wailing wall. In the aftermath, Islamic influence in the vicinity of the temple mount will increase to the point of denying Jewish access to their most sacred site – backed up by a strengthened police state in the city.

There will be an outpouring of the Spirit of God in Finland – centered in the city of Helsinki. The seeds of revival planted there in the 50's and 60's will come to fruition. Out of a legacy of piety and passion for Christ a new prophetic movement, completely disconnected from the United States will make its presence known on the world scene. Out of this movement, a new monasticism will emerge as young people who generationally have been immersed in secularism will adopt the ways and writings of the desert fathers from centuries gone by as a testimony against the tide of godlessness in their home land and sister nations. Ministers and leaders from the US and South Africa will flock to the outpouring only to be rebuffed by these young zealots who identify American revivalism and the Evangelical movement as part of the problem and not part of the solution.

A scandal of immense proportions will once again rock the intelligence world as so-called black ops sites will be exposed in Antarctica where Jihadist prisoners and political dissidents will be discovered to be held. The detention of an American citizen for over a decade will be brought to light as the impunity with which the governments of the earth have run rough shod over the rights of their citizens will be exposed afresh and anew. The intelligence organizations such as the CIA, and their European counterparts will come under much scrutiny as people march in the streets to protest the loss of their freedoms and privacy. They will be branded as anarchists in the beginning and the middle classes will applaud their suppression but they will not be silenced. The "Occupy" movement of years past will be eclipsed in scale by a new protest movement. The magnitude of this counter culture movement will demonstrate a scale of social upheaval which has not been seen since the 1960's.

After Bill Clinton's death by natural causes a Republican senator will die at the point of a gun on the steps of the Capitol. His death will spark a resurgence of conservative sentiment that has not been seen for some time in the US. This person's spouse will be appointed to fulfill their term and go on to have a successful presidential bid and become the first Republican woman to gain the White House. The Republican party she will lead to reclaim the Executive branch will be a much leaner party with a platform more focused on fiscal conservatism than hot button social issues. They will be the party of economists and pragmatists that will be welcomed to staunch the runaway entitlements of the liberal majority that will have been held for so long at this time in history.

CONCLUSION

What is the message in all of these things that have been said? Is the intent to alarm or dismay those who read this? Far from it. First and foremost, the book was not my idea. As the Father spoke, so I knew it was His directive and mandate in fact that I put these things into writing. Over the course of the year that it took to get these things put down, many of the events and precursors to these things have been reported on the national scene.

The Republican party is in complete upheaval at this time, in view of the candidacy of Donald Trump – a flamboyant outsider who has excoriated the RNC establishment and made a mockery of the party. Will he be our next president? The Father plainly told me that a woman Democrat will come to power in the next 50 years. Is that Hilary? Is that the 2016 election? I asked those questions directly and did not receive an answer. When God tells us these things it is not to give us a position to get one-up on the prognosticators who delight in rightly predicting such things as a bonifides of their prophetic prowess. I have no such intention of following in those footsteps. When I see many of the subjects God spoke to me about coming into the news at the time of this writing, it brings me to shamefacedness before my savior. Things are happening. Change is upon us. God give us the grace to humble ourselves and hear His voice. Let us pray to be positioned as part of the solution and not part of the problem in regard to God's purposes that unfold over the next half century.

One thing I know beyond all doubt is that the "sky is not falling – the kingdom is coming". Nations rise and nations fall. Cataclysm is visited on the far flung lands of the earth, and the cause of the gospel goes on. Economies roil and rumble in fiscal upheaval but God is still on the throne. What is our posture in the midst of these things? We remember the words of Jesus:

> [Mar 13:29 KJV] 29 *So ye in like manner, when ye shall see these things come to pass, know that it is nigh, [even] at the doors.*

It is not popular anymore to speak of the rapture of the church or the coming of Christ. Debate and ridicule have reduced this issue to a veritable pariah in the pulpits of the church. Yet the promise of God is sure. Something is ahead for the people of God and the nations of the earth. The affairs of men and the governments of men will grind to a halt and be brought to their knees at the foot of the cross. Will this *Parousia* take place in the next 50 years? Possibly. Perhaps even probably – yet that expectation is tempered with the reality that the Master said "I come quickly…" and yet it has been 2000 years! We then can only posture ourselves in a place of OCCUPYING till He comes. We work and plan and build like He isn't coming back for a 1000 years but we give Him permission to come back before you finish reading this sentence!

Made in the USA
Charleston, SC
19 September 2016